Theory into Practice

Sense Publishers is delighted to announce the new book series: Constructing Knowledge: Curriculum Studies in Action. We would like to invite you to submit to the series. For more information about this series or contributions, contact the Editor Brad Porfilio (porfilio16@aol.com) or Michel Lokhorst (michel.lokhorst@sensepublishers.com). We look forward to hearing from you.

CONSTRUCTING KNOWLEDGE: CURRICULUM STUDIES IN ACTION
Volume 3

Series Editors
Brad Porfilio, *Lewis University, Chicago, IL, USA*
Julie Gorlewski, *State University of New York at New Paltz, USA*
David Gorlewski, *D'Youville College, Buffalo, NY, USA*

Editorial Board
Christine Sleeter, *California State University, Monterey*
Peter McLaren, *University of California, Los Angeles*
Wayne Ross, *University of British Columbia, Canada*
Dennis Carlson, *University of Miami, Ohio*
Sue Books, *State University of New York at New Paltz*
Ken Lindblom, *Stony Brook University, Stony Brook, New York*
Eve Tuck, *State University of New York at New Paltz*

Scope
"Curriculum" is an expansive term; it encompasses vast aspects of teaching and learning. Curriculum can be defined as broadly as "The content of schooling in all its forms" (English, p. 4) and as narrowly as a lesson plan.

Complicating matters is the fact that curricula are often organized to fit particular time frames. The incompatible and overlapping notions that curriculum involves everything that is taught and learned in a particular setting *and* that this learning occurs in a limited time frame reveal the nuanced complexities of curriculum studies.

"Constructing Knowledge" provides a forum for systematic reflection on the substance (subject matter, courses, programs of study), purposes, and practices used for bringing about learning in educational settings. Of concern are such fundamental issues as: What should be studied? Why? By whom? In what ways? And in what settings? Reflection upon such issues involves an inter-play among the major components of education: subject matter; learning; teaching; and the larger social, political, and economic contexts; as well as the immediate instructional situation. Historical and autobiographical analyses are central in understanding the contemporary realties of schooling and envisioning how to (re)shape schools to meet the intellectual and social needs of all societal members. Curriculum is a social construction that results from a set of decisions; it is written and enacted, and both facets undergo constant change as contexts evolve.

This series aims to extend the professional conversation about curriculum in contemporary educational settings. Curriculum is a designed experience intended to promote learning. Because it is socially constructed, curriculum is subject to all the pressures and complications of the diverse communities that comprise schools and other social contexts in which citizens gain self-understanding.

Theory into Practice

Case Stories for School Leaders

Julie A. Gorlewski
State University of New York, New Paltz, USA

David A. Gorlewski
D'Youville College, Buffalo, USA

Thomas M. Ramming
State University of New York, Buffalo, USA

SENSE PUBLISHERS
ROTTERDAM/BOSTON/TAIPEI

A C.I.P. record for this book is available from the Library of Congress.

ISBN: 978-94-6209-047-7 (paperback)
ISBN: 978-94-6209-048-4 (hardback)
ISBN: 978-94-6209-049-1 (e-book)

Published by: Sense Publishers,
P.O. Box 21858,
3001 AW Rotterdam,
The Netherlands
https://www.sensepublishers.com/

Printed on acid-free paper

DEDICATION

For Jeffrey, Jacob, Jonathan, & Jennie – JG
For Todd & Amy – DG
For Kate – TR

Teaching, learning, and leading are all acts of love.

TABLE OF CONTENTS

ACKNOWLEDGEMENTS

If it is true (as we believe it is) that leaders shape the cultures of institutions and also that institutional cultures influence the identities of those within them, we must first express gratitude to innumerable educators who led us to love learning and leading. This book is a tribute to the principles that school leaders embody as well as the courage they inspire.

We are also grateful to those whose experiences contributed directly to this volume. Victoria Hankey, a dedicated teacher who leads through actions and words, wrote case story 4T. Teresa Lawrence, an accomplished educator and leader who stretches the boundaries of the field with energy and integrity, created case stories 2D and 6D. The stories shared by Victoria and Teresa, like all the stories in this book, are based on actual events: real people in real places struggled to understand and resolve the dilemmas you will read. These struggles, as well as the physical, psychological, and emotional energy it takes to lead institutions dedicated to human development, are honored here.

FOREWORD

Like any text, this work can be read in many different ways. With the least generosity of spirit, it may be read (dismissed) as just another example of an anachronistic leftist plea. But, I hope it will be read generously as an example and invitation for educators, *as educators*, to take back the discourses currently mediating much policy making, planning, and assessment in the field of public schooling as discourses constantly in need of grounding in an authentic vision of education. Of course, this is something in which all of us can, and need, to participate wherever we think our political affiliations lie.

Standards, accountability, effective learning, professionalism, and efficient organization are just some of the terms forming the "professional" *lingua franca* of educational leadership as it is currently practiced. But, how should we understand these terms? What are their unsaid biases and how much room do they leave for genuine intellectual and spiritual participation? This is a particularly important question at a time when professional language itself feels like it is either being deliberately co-opted to steer us along paths far removed from a genuine interest in education or simply to be drawing us, by its own unaccounted volition, into a river of educational forgetfulness.

But, it is in education that we are primarily interested. This book reminds us of that and goes some way in showing the importance of the struggle to take on educational and leadership discourses not simply as adversaries but, more importantly, as realms of unfinished business inviting constant clarification while we entertain them as sites of possibility. For example, the book reminds us that when we try to sustain a vision of education, the concept of standards should play a role quite different from standardization; that what counts as just and fair leadership might not simply be a matter of universal principle but also a matter of qualities of being with others; that what counts as effective learning might have little to do with education until "effective" is understood in humanistic and ethical ways; that what counts as professionalism might not simply be a matter of co-opting the values and meanings this term signifies when used for practices other than education, and; that what counts as efficient organization might not simply be a matter of increasing the production of some kind of commodity.

Educating involves learning – but it is much more than just learning. Educational learning must be humane and it must result in more of the humane. Perhaps it is a sign of our times that this aspect of education – how we become more human as part of our learning – is something we are prone to forget when our focus becomes preoccupied with operationalization. Hence, professional educators, if the phrase means anything, must see their work as representing education and not some rationalistic or bureaucratized reduction of it. To do this, I would argue that educators must become the caretakers (in a more phenomenologically and ontologically sensitive way) of discourses around education allowing epistemological concerns to take a back seat to ontological ones. For so long we have focused on such things as what is to be known (think of the standards movement); how quickly and effectively it can be known (think of the phrase "best practices"); how it can be shown, by measurement, that knowledge is being mastered (think of the standardized testing industry). But, such epistemologically orientated emphases are typically at the expense of the existential. That is, confronting what it *means* to be educated, what it *means* to be a teacher, and what it *means* to teach being.

This isn't the place to flesh out such particular ways of thinking about education but only to point out that the ways of participating in the unfinished business of educational discourses are necessarily multiple and varied and this book is a welcome and much needed foray into that very business. I am honored to write the foreword to this work.

Dr. Jed Hopkins, Associate Professor
School of Education
Edgewood College
1000 Edgewood College Drive
Madison, WI 53711-1997

CHAPTER 1

CONNECTING THEORY TO PRACTICE

I suppose leadership at one time meant muscles; but today it means getting along with people. Indira Gandhi

Leadership and learning are indispensable to each other. John F. Kennedy

Leadership is often mistakenly perceived as the exercise of power. Neophyte leaders may share comedian Tina Fey's (2011) misconceptions about the nature of the role: "Contrary to what I believed as a little girl, being the boss almost never involves marching around, waving your arms, and chanting, 'I am the boss! I am the boss!'" (p. 5). In reality, leaders who adopt a stance of singular righteousness may find themselves in exactly the situation Fey describes – "leading" a solitary parade accompanied only by their own declarations.

True leadership in any endeavor implies interrelations among people: leadership requires followership. In the field of education, where critical thinking is valued and fostered, blind obedience is neither desired nor likely. This reality complicates the lives of school leaders, since they cannot rely on issuing orders as a primary strategy for implementing policy or effecting change. Educational leadership is an inherently moral, principled undertaking; therefore, it is fundamentally – and purposefully – grounded in the construction of strong, positive relationships.

This introductory chapter is divided into three parts. Part 1, entitled *School Leaders, Neoliberalism, and the State of Public Education*, provides a broad context for the aspiring school leader. The challenges – and changes – in public education cannot be viewed in isolation. They are part of a neoliberal ideology that has been in the making for well over 30 years. Today's challenges are merely the fruits of that ideology. The authors argue that fundamental changes in society, particularly in relation to the free market, have redefined the very concepts of funding, purpose, and choice in public education.

Part 2 of this chapter, *Leading, Following, and Building Relationships*, discusses, from theoretical and practical perspectives, the importance of relationships as a condition for change and school improvement. While relationships, per se, do not constitute a specific leadership standard, the notion of relationships is embedded across the standards. The ability to work well with (and by that, we mean earn the respect and commitment of) staff, students, parents, and other stakeholders is critical to the effectiveness of a school leader.

Part 3 of this chapter, *Critical Analysis*, discusses two additional aspects of effective leadership: the notion that school leaders must be lifelong learners – constantly assessing and reassessing situations and decisions. This is coupled with

1

the need to develop and adhere to a leadership platform based on set of guiding beliefs about the purposes and role of education.

PART 1: SCHOOL LEADERS, NEOLIBERALISM,
AND THE STATE OF PUBLIC EDUCATION

Before engaging in the details of this text (which focuses on administrative decision-making and standards for school leaders), it is critically important to step back and assess the state of public education today. Though the future can never be predicted with certainty, a close look will reveal the challenges that educators (both administrators *and* teachers) are facing today and will face in the near future. In fact, the trajectory of change is identifiable; one merely needs to look back a few decades, and then take a snapshot of the present, in order to determine the direction of public education. Virtually all decisions made by school leaders are (and will be) affected in some way by the effects of neoliberalism (an ideology which sees schools as "markets").

Perhaps the most significant force affecting all aspects of American life in the past 30 years has been the ideology of neoliberalism (and the related implementation of neoliberal policies). In recent years, the authors of this text have worked closely with aspiring school leaders as well as experienced school administrators. We have been struck by how few have heard of neoliberalism – and how even fewer know the meaning of the term. To survive as a school leader today and in the future, we believe that knowledge and understanding of neoliberalism is a critical first step.

In 1980, free marketer Milton Friedman wrote, "The establishment of the school system in the United States is an island of socialism in a free market sea" (McLeod, 2006). It is important to note that public education, as presented by Friedman, is considered at odds with the free enterprise system. Since that point in time, public education – along with virtually every social activity – has been affected (often dramatically) by neoliberal policies. What is neoliberalism? According to David Harvey (2005), neoliberalism

> is in the first instance a theory of political economic practices that proposes that human well-being can best be advanced by liberating individual entrepreneurial freedoms and skills within an institutional framework characterized by strong private property rights, free markets and free trade. The role of the state is to... guarantee... the proper functioning of markets... [and] if markets do not exist (in areas such as... education, health care, social security and environmental pollution) then they must be created, by the state if necessary. (p. 159)

Harvey elaborates on the overall goal (as well as the means) of neoliberalism which, he notes, "seeks to bring all human action into the domain of the market. This requires technologies of information creation and capacities to accumulate, store, transfer, analyze, and use massive databases to guide decisions in the global marketplace" (p. 160).

It is impossible to separate the transformation that has occurred in public education since 1980 from the economic policies during that same period. Taubman (2009) and others have pointed out that the abiding wisdom in the last few decades is that "what is good for business is good for the world and that democracy and freedom mean free markets and the freedom to choose among consumer goods" (p. 96). What has emerged from this ideology is a set of policies which support deregulation, privatization, spending cuts, and inflation reduction (Bakan, 2004).

From the definition of neoliberalism (everything should be market-driven), to its means of operation (information accumulation and analysis), to its related policies (deregulation and privatization), an aspiring school leader can begin to see the connection between that ideology and the current state of public education. School vouchers and charter schools, along with the mandates of the federal No Child Left Behind (NCLB), and Race to the Top (RTT) legislative initiatives, are all designed to offer choice. However, each example of choice draws dollars away from public education and, in essence, moves those dollars to entities over which the public has no control. Organizations such as the American Legislative Exchange Council (ALEC), working with individual state legislatures, are drafting templates for laws which are designed to funnel tax dollars from public schools to private and/or "for profit" institutions. These private and "for profit" institutions are now receiving taxpayer support but no public oversight. Such legislation is growing exponentially with the intent of developing a market-driven education system marked by privatization and standardization.

WHY STANDARDS?

Standards, like many aspects of teaching, learning, and leading, are more complicated than they seem. Definitions and applications of standards vary; however, in general, standards function as targets or aspirations.

In this era of positivist hyper-accountability, it is important to distinguish between standards and standardization. Standards represent characteristics of significant achievement that professionals in a field should strive to attain. Standardization, on the other hand, implies common, uniform achievement – an objective that stands in opposition to the excellence signified by a standard. Standardization is associated with baseline or minimum competency goals. Standards, in contrast, epitomize ideals that may never be accomplished. In this sense, they represent continuous improvement.

In education, standards are multilayered and interrelated. Standards exist for students, for teachers, and for administrators. Moreover, teachers are evaluated, at least in part, on the basis of how *students* progress in terms of *their* assigned standards; likewise, administrators are assessed on the basis of how teachers and students perform with respect to particular standards. While this book is organized around the Interstate School Leaders Licensure Consortium (ISLLC) Standards for School Leaders Standards (Figure 1), the complications and interconnections embodied by standards are key considerations throughout.

Despite lofty aims, no set of standards is perfect. Like all aspects of teaching, learning, and leading, standards represent sets of decisions made by people. Therefore, standards necessarily embody assumptions, biases and preconceptions that the creators of the standards may not be fully aware of. This makes it necessary for educational leaders to adopt a critical stance with respect to the language of standards, as well as the tools and processes relating to the implementation of standards-based activities, curricula, and assessments. Standards may appear sensible and admirable because they align with our own worldview; this is a condition of which we should remain skeptical and wary. When reading standards and considering how they affect practice, leaders must continuously reflect on *whose interests are served, whose interests are hindered, whose perspectives are present*, and *whose perspectives are absent*.

Standard 1: An education leader promotes the success of every student by facilitating the development, articulation, implementation, and stewardship of a vision of learning that is shared and supported by all stakeholders.

Functions:
A. Collaboratively develop and implement a shared vision and mission
B. Collect and use data to identify goals, assess organizational effectiveness, and promote organizational learning
C. Create and implement plans to achieve goals
D. Promote continuous and sustainable improvement
E. Monitor and evaluate progress and revise plans

Standard 2: An education leader promotes the success of every student by advocating, nurturing, and sustaining a school culture and instructional program conducive to student learning and staff professional growth.

Functions:
A. Nurture and sustain a culture of collaboration, trust, learning, and high expectations
B. Create a comprehensive, rigorous, and coherent curricular program
C. Create a personalized and motivating learning environment for students
D. Supervise instruction
E. Develop assessment and accountability systems to monitor student progress
F. Develop the instructional and leade rship capacity of staff
G. Maximize time spent on quality instruction
H. Promote the use of the most effective and appropriate technologies to support teaching and learning
I. Monitor and evaluate the impact of the instructional program

Standard 3: An education leader promotes the success of every student by ensuring management of the organization, operation, and resources for a safe, efficient, and effective learning environment.

Functions:
A. Monitor and evaluate the management and operational systems
B. Obtain, allocate, align, and efficiently utilize human, fiscal, and technological resources
C. Promote and protect the welfare and safety of students and staff
D. Develop the capacity for distributed leadership
E. Ensure teacher and organizational time is focused to support quality instruction and student learning

Figure 1. ISLLC Standards 2008.

Standard 4: An education leader promotes the success of every student by collaborating with faculty and community members, responding to diverse community interests and needs, and mobilizing community resources.

Functions:

A. Collect and analyze data and information pertinent to the educational environment

B. Promote understanding, appreciation, and use of the community's diverse cultural, social, and intellectual resources

C. Build and sustain positive relationships with families and caregivers

D. Build and sustain productive relationships with community partners

Standard 5: An education leader promotes the success of every student by acting with integrity, fairness, and in an ethical manner.

Functions:

A. Ensure a system of accountability for every student's academic and social success

B. Model principles of self-awareness, reflective practice, transparency, and ethical behavior

C. Safeguard the values of democracy, equity, and diversity

D. Consider and evaluate the potential moral and legal consequences of decision-making

E. Promote social justice and ensure that individual student needs inform all aspects of schooling

Standard 6: An education leader promotes the success of every student by understanding, responding to, and influencing the political, social, economic, legal, and cultural context.

Functions:

A. Advocate for children, families, and caregivers

B. Act to influence local, district, state, and national decisions affecting student learning

C. Assess, analyze, and anticipate emerging trends and initiatives in order to adapt leadership strategies (Council of Chief State School Officers, pp. 14-15)

Figure 1. (Contd.). ISLLC Standards 2008.

The ISSLC Standards were developed in consultation with National Policy Board for Educational Administration (NPBEA) and the Council of Chief State School Officers (CCSSO); furthermore, they were subject to numerous rounds of revision based on open forums intended to promote and incorporate public comments from all stakeholders. According to the NPBEA, the development of the new policy standards is based on the following principles:

1. Reflect the centrality of student learning;
2. Acknowledge the changing role of the school leader;
3. Recognize the collaborative nature of school leadership;
4. Improve the quality of the profession;
5. Inform performance-based systems of assessment and evaluation for school leaders;
6. Demonstrate integration and coherence; and
7. Advance access, opportunity, and empowerment for all members of the school community. (Council of Chief State School Officers, 2008, p. 8)

It is evident that the stated intent of the standards is to benefit students, the educational profession, and society. As with any propositions that promise excellence, equity, and empowerment, these standards are both unassailable and unattainable. From a teaching-learning perspective, these problems offer fascinating challenges: *What do standards mean in practice? How can they be fostered and assessed in everyday institutions devoted to teaching and learning?* Using case story analysis, this book attempts to address these questions.

PART 2: LEADING, FOLLOWING, AND BUILDING RELATIONSHIPS

Educational institutions, historically, have been charged to achieve numerous, sometimes conflicting, goals. Expectations of stakeholders in society vary with respect to the purposes of schooling, especially when public funds are involved. The tensions around these issues are not easily resolved; indeed, they represent ongoing social debates between relatively extreme points of view. Figure 2 provides a few examples of these debates.

Schools should:	
Develop students to be law-abiding citizens who respect authority and will maintain existing social norms.	Develop students to be citizens who question authority and actively seek to transform society.
Focus on curriculum that represents accepted notions of knowledge and skills.	Focus on curriculum that challenges existing notions of knowledge and skills.
Emphasize practical academics and vocational skills that will enable learners to be productive earners.	Emphasize a comprehensive, liberal arts education that endeavors to cultivate scholarly dispositions.

Figure 2. Conflicting Purposes of Schools.

Educational leaders must be cognizant of these competing goals, as well as thoughtful about how their own practices relate to the larger social contexts in which they function. It may seem as though daily obligations have little to do with laws, policies, and cultural production; however, all political change has local effects – and all local actions have the potential to influence society. Naturally, educational leaders hope to enact positive change in accordance with their visions. But how can they do this?

FROM PAPER TO PEOPLE

Management is doing things right; leadership is doing the right things. Peter Drucker

Educational institutions, like societies, consist of people. And, while allegiance to the ideals of justice and reason are critical to the integrity of a leader, real organizational change requires dedication to building *relationships* with *people* "…based on a common commitment to the notion that ideas are more important than personalities" (Reeves, 2009 p. 3). Historically, the field of educational administration has sought to balance practical knowledge, professional knowledge, and academic knowledge (Berry & Beach, 2009). These categories, however, are not divisible. Their boundaries are blurred and their contents are intertwined. In fact, academics often claim that nothing is as practical as a good theory.

Berry and Beach (2009) describe three constructs that have shaped the development of educational administration as a field:

1. Educational administration evolved out of a need to operate schools under a set of practical and applied administrative skills.
2. The bureaucratization of educational organizations during the 19th and 20th centuries required specialized professional knowledge in order to become, and to succeed as, an educational leader.
3. The academic, scientific, and theory basis for educational administration provided educational leaders with advanced tools, conceptual frameworks, and contemporary and theoretical knowledge required to lead educational organizations. (p. 1)

As theoretical knowledge has become a more valued aspect of educational leadership, conceptual frameworks have become more valued, as well. Conceptual frameworks attempt to explain the diversity of human experiences and understandings in ways that are grounded in, and expand on, established research. Drawing on a wealth of scholarship, DeVore and Martin (2008) elaborate on these ideas and trace the shift from ethics of justice (based on external, static principles) to an ethic of care (based on relationships):

Contrasting with the ethics of justice is feminist moral theory which is grounded in the perspective of human relationships and an ethic of care (Walker, 2003). As explained by Beck and Murphy (1997), "Scholars in this camp stress the importance of developing acute moral perception, or understanding persons and context, and of cultivating virtues" (p. 33), thus, this view embraces feminist moral theory by emphasizing "caring for individuals as unique persons" (Furman, 2003, p. 3). Decision-making practices, linked with an ethic of care, are focused on relationships and the "absolute regard for the dignity and intrinsic value of each person..." (Furman, p. 3)

Proponents of feminist moral theory espouse an ethic of care and relationship-building (Beck, 1994; Noddings, 1993; Walker, 2003). Beck determined that the expectations of political leaders, teachers, and parents have created "divergent perspectives on educational purposes and on the role of administrators in fulfilling these purposes" (p. 58) which may be addressed through an ethic of care. Beck posited that "an ethic of care has the potential to provide a solid foundation" (p. 58) to meet the challenges facing administrators. (Conceptual Underpinning, para. 2).

It is essential for leaders to appreciate the importance of relationship-building from a scholarly, theoretical perspective. More notable, however, is the impact that this approach can have on the quality of the learning community. Although effects may be difficult to quantify, knowledge and awareness of this perspective are invaluable.

LEADERSHIP: TRANSFORMATIONAL, MORAL, DISTRIBUTED

It is better to lead from behind and to put others in front, especially when you celebrate victory when nice things occur. You take the front line when there is danger. Then people will appreciate your leadership. Nelson Mandela

In addition to a scholarly perspective, it is important for current and aspiring leaders to understand the importance of relationships from a practical perspective. Leithwood and Poplin (1992), borrowing from Saranson (1990), state "the predictable failure of education reform rests, in large measure, on existing power relationships in schools: relationships among teachers and administrators, parents and school staffs, students and teachers" (p. 8). Instead of power derived from title or position, Leithwood and Poplin suggest relationships where power is derived from consent.

(This) form of power (is) manifested *through* other people, not *over* other people. Such power arises, for example, when teachers are helped to find greater meaning in their work, to meet higher-level needs through their work, and to develop enhanced instructional capacities. Facilitative power arises also as school staff members learn how to make the most of their collective capacities in solving school problems. This form of power is limited, practically speaking, and substantially enhances the productivity of the school on behalf of its students. (p. 9)

Such a concept is consistent with the idea of transformational leadership where the first goal is "...helping staff members develop and maintain a collaborative, professional school culture" (p. 9). This type of culture is captured by ISLLC Standard 2, which will be discussed in chapter four.

The idea that real power is derived from consent can also be found in other literature that addresses educational leadership. Sergiovanni (2003) suggests that the real power of a leader can be measured by the commitment of followers to an idea or vision, also known as a moral purpose. In discussing followership, he states that

Followers are people committed to purposes, a cause, a vision of what the school is and can become, beliefs about teaching and learning, values and standards to which they adhere, and convictions...In other words, followership requires an emotional commitment to a set of ideas. Once in place, an idea structure constitutes the basis of a leadership practice based on professional and moral authority. (p. 71)

While Sergiovanni acknowledges that other sources of power, i.e., "bureaucratic", "psychological", and "technical-rational" (pp. 36–37) have their place, he posits that "moral authority" will result in a community of teachers whose "…performance is expansive and sustained" (pp. 36–37). This concept of moral authority led to what Sergiovanni calls moral leadership.

Distributed leadership is different from either moral or transformational leadership, but continues to build upon the themes of relationships and consent wherein teachers are viewed as willing followers rather than obedient subordinates. Spillane (2005) explains:

> A distributed perspective frames leadership practice in a particular way; leadership practice is viewed as a product of the interactions of school leaders, *followers* (emphasis added), and their situation. This point is especially important, and one that is frequently glossed over in discussions of distributed leadership. Rather than viewing leadership practice as a product of a leader's knowledge and skill, the distributed perspective defines it as the interactions between people and their situation. These interactions, rather than any particular action, are critical in understanding leadership practice. (p. 144)

The importance of effective interactions and, implicitly, the building of effective relationships, are critical to this concept of leadership.

Whether discussing transformational, moral, or distributed leadership, this point should be made: focusing on *relationships* and building a *community of followers* (based on a commitment to ideas) are essential to the practice of effective school leadership.

PART 3: CRITICAL ANALYSIS

> The first people had questions, and they were free. The second people had answers, and they became enslaved. Wind Eagle, American Indian Chief

Leadership has no template. The dispositions that result in effective leadership strategies are neither linear nor precise. Leaders enact sets of behaviors that range from improvisation to allegiance while modeling integrity of purpose. How are these contradictions possible? And what do they mean for educational leaders?

The answers lie in questions.

Authentic, high-quality leadership is characterized by continuous analysis. A good leader, then, can be described as one who is dedicated to the ideal of *continuous becoming*. This concept, suitably framed in the field of education, requires commitment to the ongoing examination of one's actions, decisions, and assumptions. In short, it requires a commitment to being a lifelong learner – in the scholarly sense of the term. In addition to the obligation to maintain a critical disposition, this approach requires a responsibility to engage with (as both *consumer* and *producer*) emerging ideas in the field relating to research, policy, and practice.

A critical framework should not be confused with "critique" or "criticism." It is, in fact, far more nuanced because consideration must be given to multilayered contexts and their interrelations. Furthermore, a critical analytical framework is not intended to generate an "answer key" or solution table. Rather, it is proposed as a means of conducting deliberations in order to connect experiences, uncover assumptions, untangle beliefs, reveal biases, and identify relevant information. Critical to this framework is the ability to ask the "right" questions before seeking the "right" answers.

What does this mean, in practice? First, as you use the framework, begin to think about and collect relevant information about the case story. Just as importantly, note what additional information, not found in the story, would be useful and significant. Make note of your preliminary assumptions and responses, but do not simply accept them. Consider alternative perspectives, and reflect on the foundations of your initial assumptions and responses. Second, make connections to research and scholarship in the field. Seek guidance from established sources, as well as emerging scholars and new research. Appreciate the shifting context of the field of education as an opportunity to model the professional disposition of lifelong learning. Third, as you encounter dilemmas in your practice, imagine the case story framework and evaluate your leadership processes in that context.

A-PIE: A CASE STORY ANALYSIS FRAMEWORK

A-PIE is an acronym for Assess, Plan, Implement, and Evaluate. The A-PIE framework was designed by the authors of this book to help readers thoroughly and consistently analyze the case stories presented. It can also be applied to "real world" dilemmas.

When applying A-PIE to case stories, the focus should be on the steps "A" and "P", but consideration must also be given to steps "I" and "E" as they are integral to the successful application of the framework. Because others may have information and perspectives that can help inform the process, we suggest that the A-PIE framework be applied to each story in collaboration with a partner or partners. In "real world" settings, those partners could include: teachers, students, parents, board of education members, peers, supervisors, and community members. Such collaboration will increase their commitment to addressing the dilemma.

Moving methodically through the A-PIE process enables school leaders to listen, question, evaluate, and learn. This will enhance the success of their plans and the validity of their decisions. Most importantly, it will support a leadership approach based on collaboration and continuous improvement.

A – Assess. Gather and assess the information presented in the case story and other information that may be pertinent. It is important to ask the right questions. For example, if the story involves a legal issue, what federal or state laws or regulations pertain to the situation? Or, if the story involves a funding issue, what literature regarding school finance is relevant? In other words, look inside and outside the story for additional information. Use questions to develop a clear understanding of the problems and possible causes.

P – Plan. Using the information that has been gathered, develop a variety of short- and long-term actions that could be implemented to address the problem. A short-term plan might involve a decision that takes just a few minutes to arrive at; a long-term plan could involve numerous committees and multi-year phases. Once again, asking the right questions is key. For example:

 a. What are the pros and cons of each action, including possible unin-tended consequences?
 b. What resources are needed?
 c. Who will be affected? What stakeholders will benefit, and how? What stakeholders will suffer, and how?

After careful deliberation, choose the actions to be taken and use them to develop a plan for addressing the problem. Next, ask more questions such as,

 a. How will we define success?
 b. How will the results or success of the plan be evaluated, both short- and long-term?
 c. What evidence will be used and how will this evidence be generated?
 d. When will evaluation take place and who will be involved?
 e. Prior to implementation, will the plan be shared with others? If so, how and when?

I – Implement. Implement and monitor the plan. Here, be sure to assign responsibility for guiding and directing the implementation of the plan to one or more individuals.

E – Evaluate. Following the steps in the plan, conduct formative and summative evaluations of the plan. Is the execution of the plan having the intended consequences? Have any unintended consequences manifested? If so, does the plan need to be modified?

Figure 3. A-PIE Steps.

CONNECTING CASE STORY ANALYSIS TO A LEADERSHIP PLATFORM

Case stories, and the results of their analyses, are not meant to remain encapsulated in an academic forum. The purpose of the endeavor is to inform practice and enhance the ongoing development of professional leadership knowledge, skills, and dispositions. A concrete way to approach this is to connect case story analysis to a leadership platform.

Developing a leadership platform enables school leaders to consider philosophical questions that influence their actions and decisions. Platforms identify and reflect deeply held values, understandings, and beliefs about leaders themselves, about education, and about the role of leadership. The development of a platform enables practitioners to merge experiences, theory, and practice by making connections between daily decisions and the larger social context that influences, and is influenced by, actors within organizations.

Leadership platforms in the field of education generally explore perspectives related to the following:

- Purpose of education
- Role of the teacher
- Role of the administrator
- Nature of the learner

When addressing these concepts, leaders should make connections to theories and to scholars who reflect the development of their beliefs, as well as consider personal and professional experiences that have influenced them. Often developed within templates specified by educational administration programs, platforms constitute an embodiment of values and mental models. Not meant to be static, they necessarily represent a point in time with respect to the dynamic process of leadership development.

DeVore and Martin (2008), referencing others in the literature, explain how personal leadership platforms can be used to address challenging situations – specifically, the tensions present in managing dilemmas:

> Beck and Murphy (1997) argued that leaders are challenged to "look within themselves, at their own values, beliefs, commitments, biases, and assumptions to assist them in managing dilemmas…" (p. 191). Other researchers suggested that leaders need to develop a platform in which to articulate their belief system (Covey, 1990; Kahn, 1990; Sergiovanni & Starratt, 1983).

In responding to the case stories, it important to integrate the A-PIE framework through a personal leadership platform, strengthening the connection between how leaders think, what they believe, and how they act.

The apparent polarization between seeking internal guidance and referring to an external[1] document such as a platform can be reconciled, in part, by engaging with case stories. This can be accomplished by associating case story analysis to the leadership platform, thereby strengthening and extending connections between theory and practice.

HOW TO USE THIS BOOK

This book is intended to complicate and animate standards to enable leaders to enhance their practice in ways that link to established theoretical perspectives. In planning this text, we wanted to recognize and validate the fact that leaders emerge at all levels of an organization, regardless of their titles. Furthermore, similar administrative titles can involve different responsibilities in different organizations. Finally, we acknowledge that authority, responsibility, and resource allocation vary tremendously across and within educational institutions.

Therefore, we decided to explore the application and implementation of ISLLC Standards through case stories that address *multiple levels of leadership*. Each standard is illustrated through three case stories: Teacher Leader, Building Leader, and District Leader. These terms are intentionally vague. Teacher leaders might be full-time or part-time positions and could include department chairs, library or learning center directors, school counselors, coaches, music/art directors, technology liaisons, and reassigned district level positions. Building leaders might include principals, assistant principals, deans, headmasters, and professional development specialists. District leaders would, of course, include superintendents; however, they could also be assistant superintendents, human resources administrators, transportation and technology coordinators, athletic directors, special education administrators, fund raisers, and grant writers. Although the stories are conveyed from these different but overlapping perspectives, the dilemmas they raise will relate to leaders in all these positions. In addition, the multiple perspectives are meant to extend the thinking of leaders at various levels so that they will approach complicated situations with greater empathy and understanding.

We suggest, therefore, that leaders at all levels read, reflect on, and apply the A-PIE analytic framework to each of the stories. In group settings, it can be helpful to role-play the stories, since leadership is not a purely cognitive undertaking. Role-playing scenarios allows participants to connect with their own feelings, assumptions, and autobiographies in ways that isolated reading and writing cannot replicate. Consider, also, how the stories relate to daily experiences and how these experiences are echoed in the larger purposes of education. All the case stories are fictionalized versions of *real events*; they illustrate issues that we have not solved, but that we continue to attempt to understand. We invite you to do the same.

NOTE

[1] Of course, a leadership platform is individually developed and, as such, is not entirely "external." However, it is distanced, at least temporally, from most dilemmas faced in the field.

REFERENCES

Bakan, J. (2004). The corporation: the pathological pursuit of profit and power. Toronto: Viking Canada.

Beck, L. G. (1994). Reclaiming educational administration as a caring profession. New York, NY: Teachers College Press.

Beck, L. G., & Murphy, J. (1997). Ethics in educational leadership programs: Emerging models. Columbia, MO: The University Council for Educational Administration.

Berry, J., & Beach, R. (2009). *K-12 leadership and the educational administration curriculum: A theory of preparation*. Retrieved from the Connexions Web site: http://cnx.org/content/m13772/1.2/

Council of Chief State School Officers. (2008). Educational leadership policy standards: ISLLC 2008. Washington, DC, United States. Retrieved from http://www.ccsso.org/Documents/2008/Educational_ Leadership_Policy_Standards_2008.pdf

Covey, S. (1990). The seven habits of highly effective people: Restoring the character ethic. New York, NY: Simon & Schuster.

DeVore, S. & Martin, B. (2008). Ethical decision-making: Practices of female and male superintendents. Advancing Women in Leadership Archives, 28(3). Retrieved 1/21/12 from http://advancingwomen .com/awl/awl_wordpress/.

Fey, T. (2011). Bossypants. NewYork, NY: ReaganArthurBooks.

CHAPTER 1

Furman, G. C. (2003). Moral leadership and the ethic of community. University Park, PA: Pennsylvania State University, Rock Ethics Institute. Retrieved July 13, 2005, from http://www.ed.psu.edu/uceacsle/VEEA/VEEA_vol2num1.pdf

Harvey, D. (2005). A brief history of neoliberalism. Oxford University Press.

Kahn, W. (1990). Toward an agenda for business ethics research. Academy of Management *Review, 15*(2), 311–328.

Leithwood, K. & Poplin, M. S. (1992). The move toward transformational leadership. *Educational leadership, 49*(5), 8–12.

McLeod, A. (2006). Great conservative minds: a condensation of Milton and Rose Friedman's *Free to Choose*. Alabama Policy Institute, Birmingham, Alabama, February.

Noddings, N. (1993). Caring: A feminist perspective. In K. A. Strike and P. L. Ternasky (Eds.), The ethics of school administration (2nd ed., pp. 43–53). New York, NY: Teachers College Press.

Reeves, D. (2009). Leading change in your school. Alexandria, VA: ASCD.

Saranson, S. B. (1990). The predictable failure of educational reform. San Francisco; Jossey-Bass.

Sergiovanni, T., & Starratt, R. (1983). Supervision: Human perspectives (3rd ed.). New York, NY: McGraw-Hill.

Spillane, J. P. (2005). *Distributed leadership*. The educational forum, *69*(2), 147–153. Retrieved May 21, 2012 from http://www.coe.iup.edu/principal/Spring%202012%20Articles/Spillane.pdf.

Taubman, P.M. (2009). Audit culture. *Deconstructing the discourse of Standards and Accountability in Education: Teaching by Numbers*. Routledge, New York and London.

Walker, M. U. (2003). Moral contexts. Lanham, MD: Rowman & Littlefield Publishers. Webster's American College Dictionary. 1998. NY: Random House.

STANDARD 1: VISIONS OF LEARNING

Standard 1: *A school administrator is an educational leader who promotes the success of all students by facilitating the development, articulation, implementation, and stewardship of a vision of learning that is shared and supported by the school community.*

Functions:

A.   *Collaboratively develop and implement a shared vision and mission*
B.   *Collect and use data to identify goals, assess organizational effectiveness, and promote organizational learning*
C.   *Create and implement plans to achieve goals*
D.   *Promote continuous and sustainable improvement*
E.   *Monitor and evaluate progress and revise plans*

A vision is a representation of the possible. It is a guiding philosophy – a linguistic attempt to fuse theory and practice, the real and the ideal. Clearly, the development of a mental image that unites esoteric aspirations with authentic actualities is not easy. Northouse (2009) explains that effective leadership entails a recursive process of multiple phases. Drawing on research about leadership, he notes that "visions have five characteristics: a picture, a change, values, a map, and a challenge" (p. 88).

While the development of a vision of learning is a collaborative venture, the first phase involves establishing a personal vision. Although this may seem to be an individual task, the development of a personal vision requires dynamic interactions within various contexts, both inside and outside of educational institutions. Robbins and Alvy (2004), using the role of building principal as the representation of an individual leader, describe the contextual interrelations that affect, and are affected by, the development of a personal vision:

> Roland Barth defines leadership as "making happen what you believe in" (2001, p. 446). This is accomplished through symbolic and expressive leadership behaviors. From the symbolic perspective, a principal models and focuses individual attention on what is important. From the expressive side of leadership, principals talk with teachers, help to crystallize and communicate the rationale for a vision, and generate shared discussions about what is important in the school. This focus on the meaning of a school leads to the development of a mission statement grounded in the collective

beliefs of the staff. The process creates a commitment to a common direction and generates energy to pursue it. But it begins with a personal leadership vision. (p. 6)

Personal visions are developed over time, after significant investments in deliberation, contemplation, and conversation. It is essential that one's personal vision embodies morals, values, and beliefs that aspire to the best imaginable future. Northouse (2009) clarifies this phase:

A competent leader will have a compelling vision that challenges people to work toward a higher standard of excellence. A vision is a mental model of an ideal future state. It provides a *picture* (all emphases in original) of a future that is better than the present, is grounded in *values*, and advocates *change* toward some new set of ideals. Visions function as a *map* to give people direction. Visions also *challenge* people to commit themselves to a greater common good. (p. 98)

Once a personal vision has been established, ideally in a shared context, that vision must be communicated to extend throughout the learning community. As in any exchange of ideas, sharing a vision involves potential for bonding and growth as well as conflict and misunderstanding. Therefore, the communicative process must be painstaking, conscientious, and committed to transparent expressive and receptive interactions. Northouse (2009) describes the complexity of articulating one's vision:

First, an effective leader clearly articulates the vision to others. This requires the leader to adapt the vision to the attitudes and values of the audience. Second, the leader highlights the intrinsic values of the vision, emphasizing how the vision presents ideals worth pursuing. Third, a competent leader uses language that is motivating and uplifting to articulate the vision. Finally, the leader uses inclusive language that enlists participation from others and builds community. (p. 98)

Drawing on Hirsch (1996), Robbins and Arvy (2004) specify the importance of moving effectively from a personal vision to a vision that is shared by the educational community.

A school vision should be a descriptive statement of what the school will be like at a specified time in the future. It uses descriptive words or phrases and sometimes pictures to illustrate what one would expect to see, hear, and experience in the school at that time. It engages all stakeholders in answering such questions as:

- What kind of school do we want for our children and staff?
- What will students learn? How will they learn?
- How will students benefit from attendance at our school?
- How will their success be measured or demonstrated?

- Of all the educational innovations and research, which strategies should we seek to employ in our school?
- If parents had a choice, on what basis would they choose to send their children to our school? (Hirsch, cited in Robbins and Alvy, np)

The final phase related to visionary leadership involves implementation – moving from words to actions that reflect and inform policies and practices. Once again, Northouse (2009) links this phase to the characteristics of a vision:

A challenge for a leader is to carry out the difficult processes of implementing a vision. To implement a vision, the leader needs to be a living *model* (all emphases in original) of the ideals and values articulated in the vision. In addition, he or she must *set high performance expectations* for others, and *encourage and empower* others to reach their goals. (p. 98)

In practice, this phase often involves the creation of a mission statement. Hirsch (1996) offers key ideas for getting started:

A mission statement is a succinct, powerful statement on how the school will achieve its vision. The mission answers:

- What is our purpose?
- What do we care most about?
- What must we accomplish?
- What are the cornerstones of our operations? (Hirsch, cited in Robbins and Alvy, 2004, np)

A clear, concise mission statement provides a representation of the learning community to which the group aspires. It is developed in collaboration with all stakeholders and reflects the values, hopes, and dreams of all learners. But, as important as the mission and vision statements are, a vision is more than words. It is an embodiment of ideas and morals of an ideal society, and its underlying philosophies are a guide for decision making, in both macro and micro contexts. A vision presents the priorities of leaders and links those priorities to the expectations of the communities they serve.

CASE STORY 1T: TEACHER LEADER

Although they appeared to be polar opposites in every respect, principal Rick DeJesus and assistant principal Bob Saunders worked amazingly well together. Rick, only 29, was in his first year as principal after having served for a short period of time as a middle school social studies teacher and as a "teacher-on-special-assignment" (referred to as a TOSA) for curriculum development. In that capacity, Rick had conducted in-service training sessions on the latest state and national initiatives and had led teams of teachers in developing new curriculum guides. He was effective and popular. When the principal position had opened up at Choctaw Middle School, Rick was the rumored "odds on" favorite to get the position – and the odds-makers had proven to be correct.

In contrast to Rick's meteoric rise from 7th grade social studies teacher, to a TOSA, to a building principal, Bob Saunders had been the assistant at Choctaw for over 25 years. He was good at his job, was considered the quintessential middle manager and, most importantly, was quite happy with his position as assistant principal. While Rick, by nature, was ambitious, intellectually curious, deeply reflective, and eager to embrace new ideas, Bob saw himself as the steady, dependable administrator who, as he often reminded colleagues, "kept the ship afloat." In reality, both types of leadership were critically important in running any organization and the fact that the two men worked so well together was, in a sense, a compliment to each.

In their first year together, Rick found Bob's knowledge of organizational culture and his no-nonsense approach to student discipline indispensable to the effective operation of the school. And, though Rick was young enough to be Bob's son, Bob was impressed with Rick's enthusiasm. Moreover, their professional relationship was strengthened by the respect Rick showed for Bob's perspective on everything from conducting assemblies to developing agendas for staff meetings.

Choctaw Middle School social worker Denise Stapleton held a unique position in terms of respect and authority. Both attributes were enhanced by her close professional relationship with the two building administrators. Denise's first five years as Choctaw's social worker had been a bit frustrating. She was originally hired because the school was undergoing significant demographic changes in the composition of the student body, particularly with respect to socio-economic status. The proportion of Choctaw students on the federal "Free and Reduced Lunch" program had risen from 12% to 41% within ten years; school suspensions were up, and standardized test scores were down. District leaders had determined that a social worker was needed to mediate the growing problems between and among students, teachers, social service agencies, and (at times) local police.

Unfortunately, despite the clear need for her services, Denise had felt invisible in her first years on the job. Rick's predecessor, the now retired Tom Daley, had seemed to have no time for her. Though he claimed to have faith in her abilities, he'd rarely responded to any of her written reports and was dismissive whenever they'd met to discuss a student issue. Therefore, Denise had been excited when she learned that Rick DeJesus would be the new principal. Her hopes had risen even more when Rick singled out Denise at his first staff meeting and announced how happy he was to have a social worker in his school. He had mentioned that he would be depending on her to offer advice and direction in dealing with difficult student issues. Back on that warm day in late August, neither Denise nor Rick, nor even Bob for that matter, had realized how quickly her expertise would be tested.

The student's name was Steven Hicks. He was an 8th grader who had entered Choctaw Middle School in grade 6. His record as a student during this time was not unusual in any way. However, things changed in late October. In an effort to build morale and strengthen connections among teachers and students, Rick suggested that the school sponsor an "Opposite Day." A committee of teachers and students put together the program and Rick was delighted with the results: suggestions were made to reverse the class schedule for the day, to serve lunch beginning with dessert, to make teachers carry hall passes, and to allow cross-gender attire.

When "Opposite Day" arrived, Rick was pleased to see that the entire school – teachers, students, and support staff – participated. Everyone seemed to embrace the spirit of "Opposite Day." Perhaps the most entertaining aspect of the event was the number of boys who dressed as girls. Generally, the boys made caricatures of their perceptions of femininity, exaggerating the ways girls dress, walk, and wear make-up. But not Steven Hicks.

Steven was the talk of the school because, although he also chose to dress as a girl, he did so in the most deliberate way; that is to say, he took the time to find girls' clothing that made it difficult for observers to identify him as a boy. And, unlike the caricatures presented by the other boys, Steven's performance was authentic – right down to the curled hair, carefully applied make-up, stylish purse and high heels.

All of this would have been a footnote for the school year except that Steven showed up for school the next day again dressed as a girl. His homeroom teacher, feeling that Steven's dress was "inappropriate," sent him to the office, where he was confronted by Bob Saunders.

Bob had seen many things in his years as an assistant principal, but this situation was new. He asked Steven why he was dressed this way. The eighth grader, without hesitating, said he had always felt like a girl and that from now on he planned to look like one. He said his clothing on "Opposite Day" made him feel "right" for the first time in his life and that he never wanted to lose that feeling again. Bob asked Steven if his parents knew how he had dressed for school and Steven said that they knew – and that they didn't care. For the first time in his career, Bob felt like he was out of his league; so he presented the situation to Rick.

Rick met with Steven and came away impressed with the student's sense of certainty that he was a girl in a boy's body – and that he only felt "normal" when dressed in girls' clothing. Rick pointed out to Steven that other people – in this case, students – might be less tolerant. Did he know what he was getting into? Steven was adamant. This was his choice.

Rick's vision of a healthy, productive and safe school environment meant that diversity – in all its forms – was to be nurtured and embraced. Rick thought back to his own days in middle school and high school and remembered them as difficult. He recalled how hard it was to fit in and was determined that Choctaw Middle would allow every student to feel the sense of belonging that he felt was essential for academic success. At the end of the meeting, Rick asked Steven to meet with the school's social worker. That was when Denise got involved.

Denise met with Steven later that day and continued meeting with him daily for several weeks. She also arranged to have him see a therapist. Denise was moved by Steven's descriptions of his hidden identity, how he craved girls' clothing, and how desperately he wanted to be accepted. She even brought in some of her own garments – scarves, shoes, and accessories – to show support for Steven.

In the meantime, Steven continued to dress as a girl. As the principal, Rick wanted to support Steven. He conducted staff meetings around this topic, encouraging teachers to accept Steven's behaviors and to ask their students to do the same.

Bob suggested that they suspend him from school until he "dressed appropriately," but the school district's attorney noted that there was no law prohibiting a boy from dressing as a girl; in fact, the state's hate-crime law prevented gender discrimination.

Things were relatively quiet for awhile. But then Steven's attire became more flamboyant. His clothing became more provocative. Regular shoes were replaced by spike heels. Dresses became shorter, and the make-up heavier. Students, particularly the boys, began to ridicule him. When a social studies teacher assigned students to work in groups, one of the students in Steven's group refused to participate, declaring, "I'm not gonna be in the same group with that freak!" Teachers reported a growing number of students talking about Steven and commenting sarcastically on his daily appearance.

Rick decided to call a meeting with Bob and Denise to discuss the situation and develop an approach that would serve the best interests of both Steven and the rest of the school.

"Ok," said Rick. Let's go around the table and lay out our concerns about Steven Hicks."

Denise started. "My heart goes out to this boy. His identity is deeply embedded in his belief that he is a girl. From what I know about this type of situation – and the therapist supports it – we cannot change him. I know that some students don't want to be near him…but that's their problem, not Steven's. There was time when students with special needs were not welcomed into regular classrooms, and we now know that that wasn't right. Aren't we supposed to be teaching more than just academic stuff? What happened to tolerance, diversity, social justice?"

Rick turned to Bob.

Bob, deep in thought, was staring out the window of Rick's office. He was watching a work crew apply a protective coating on the surface of the school's asphalt parking lot.

"I don't know," he began slowly. "I mean, you both know where I stand on this. I thought that he should have been suspended after we warned him about the impression he was making. But we were told that our hands are tied – that he has a 'right' to dress as he pleases and that we might be violating the 'hate-crime' law. Well, what about the rights of the rest of the students? As I see it, our students have a right to an education free from distractions. That's my problem with this whole situation. Just think of the number of meetings we've had because of this kid: administrative time, staff meetings, reports to the Superintendent, meetings with the therapist. I mean… come on, already. What he's doing is 'in your face' defiant behavior – and it's getting worse. Mark my words: he's going to take it another step. It's just a matter of time."

Bob paused, then continued.

"We can't suspend him for dressing like a girl? Fine. So, let's take disciplinary action against him for being a distraction – for preventing other kids from getting an education."

The group fell silent. Bob and Denise both turned toward Rick. Denise broke the silence.

"So," she asked. "What are we going to do?"

CASE STORY 1B: BUILDING LEADER

Sharon White was enjoying her fourth year as principal at King Elementary School in Rockville County. King Elementary, 1 of 24 K-8 schools in the district, served a diverse and relatively poor population. When Sharon had been appointed as principal, over 70% of the students in 8th grade scored below the state benchmark for proficiency on both the math and literacy assessments. The results for students in 4th grade were similar.

However, over the past three years scores had steadily improved and now more than 80% of the 4th and 8th graders achieved proficiency on state tests. This turnaround was not accidental; it was largely the result of two variables – the appointment of Sharon White as principal and the fact that the school had been "adopted" by a local financial corporation, Niagara Capital, which provided significant additional support to the school.

Sharon had begun her career as a reading teacher in an affluent suburban district, but after a few years recognized that she wanted to return to her roots in Rockville. So, after gaining tenure in her initial position, she took a job as a reading coach in the large Rockville school district and began her studies leading to administrative certification. Five years later, at the relatively young age of 31, she was appointed principal at King Elementary.

Much had changed since Sharon had graduated from Rockville High School. Like many "rustbelt" cities around the Great Lakes, Rockville had continued to experience a loss of well-paying blue collar jobs, a loss that had led to urban flight and decay. Unemployment in the community hovered around 20%. Currently, the dwindling population of Rockville was 46% African-American, 31% Hispanic, and 22% white. Most of the students came from families who had resettled in the city after escaping civil wars, famines and natural disasters that plagued their villages in Africa and Central America. State reports indicated that students who entered the high school in 9th grade had only a 50% chance of graduating.

King Elementary served a significant number of students whose families had resettled in Rockville as well as large number of African-American and Hispanic students. Twenty-five percent of the students were English language learners and the poverty rate was near 80%. Despite these demographics, Sharon, with financial support from Niagara Capital, had been able to lead the turnaround of the school and King Elementary was being hailed as one of the bright spots in the city.

Many of the other elementary schools in the district, on the other hand, were labeled as "persistently low achieving" – a designation for schools which experienced overall poor performance on state tests for three consecutive years.

Therefore, the state was now requiring the district to take what was referred to as "corrective action." This process included the development of a district-wide improvement plan. In some cases, principals had to be replaced and over 50% of the teachers had to be removed from the school. Failure to meet these requirements would cause the loss of millions of dollars in state aid for the district, something it certainly could not afford.

Sharon was sitting in her office one afternoon late in the school year when she received an unexpected visit from the school district superintendent, Dr. William James.

"Sharon, sorry to barge in like this, but do you have a minute?" William asked.

Although surprised by the superintendent's visit, Sharon welcomed him. "Sure Dr. James. Please come in Can I get you a soda or cup of coffee?"

"No thanks Sharon – not right now. I've got something important to share with you." He paused and leaned forward.

"You know you have done a great job here at King. Parents, teachers and students all love you, and – under your leadership – students are learning and achieving. Even the local paper, which is not very friendly toward our schools, sings your praises. You have a lot to be proud of... and I have a favor to ask."

Noting Sharon's quizzical expression, William lifted his chin and tapped it with his index finger, then continued speaking.

"Well, I guess it's really not a favor. Let me explain. As you know, three of our elementary schools have been labeled "persistently low achieving" and the state has directed us to make changes. I have discussed this at length with the school board and the central office administrators and we have come to the conclusion that we have no choice. We must follow the state's directives. We have to replace the three principals assigned to the low achieving schools and shift 50% of their teachers to other schools. These actions will require sacrifices across the board, from everyone involved. The bottom line, Sharon, is this: we want you to take over as principal of Ashland Elementary."

Sharon's shoulders dropped and she swallowed hard before meeting the superintendent's steady gaze. "Dr. James," said Sharon, "Ashland is the lowest performing school in the district."

"I know," said the superintendent, "but we all feel strongly that you can make a difference."

After a few seconds – and a deep breath – Sharon responded. "Dr. James, I'm flattered that you think I can perform miracles, but my heart belongs to the students, staff and parents at King. Together, we've created a vision of what we wanted the school to be and I believe we have made remarkable progress toward making that vision a reality. However, we still have a long way to go. While 80% of our students are achieving proficiency, 20% are not. Our vision statement says that 90% of students will achieve proficiency within five years – that's less than two years from now. I want to continue to build on what we've started. And, besides –"

Dr. James interrupted. "Sharon, this is not a request. I'm not giving you a choice. We need to put a proven leader, a difference-maker, at the helm at

Ashland, and you're that person. All of us have supreme confidence in you. You're bright, you know the city, you relate well to parents, you can engage with diverse populations, and you inspire teachers. Sharon, people want to work for you."

"But, Dr. James," said Sharon, "the problems at Ashland are so deeply embedded that they seem almost... insurmountable. The building is in terrible condition, the neighborhood is run down and crime-ridden, attendance rates are among the worst in the city; and the faculty is, perhaps, *too* experienced. They are too far into their careers to even think about changing. I don't see how replacing even 50% of the teachers will make much of a difference, because those who remain will likely poison the attitudes of the new staff members."

"Sharon, I understand your concerns – but our plan requires you to start at Ashland on July 1. Begin thinking about who you'd like as assistant principal, as well as the process you're going to use to hire 24 new teachers – that's exactly half the staff. Those teachers must come from voluntary transfers or displacements from other buildings. Remember, you are mandated to follow the teachers' contract. The district's human resources department can help you there. Also, I want you to consider the importance of engaging the entire school community in this turnaround. Sharon, I know you're up to this. We're all counting on you."

With those words, William James stood, shook her hand warmly, and left.

Sitting alone in her office, Sharon White was devastated. She was proud of what she had accomplished at King and had developed close ties with the school. Sharon appreciated the vote of confidence by her administrative superiors. But the superintendent's decision made her wonder if she would have been better off being a *less* effective leader. Ashland's problems dwarfed those she had faced at King, and the economy meant that business partnerships were unlikely to emerge.

Sharon couldn't help but ask herself: "Have my successes, somehow, set me up for failure?"

CASE STORY 1D: DISTRICT LEADER

Superintendent Emma Howard straightened her skirt and buttoned her jacket as she prepared to address Warsaw High School's National Honor Society inductees and their proud parents. It was one of her favorite evening activities – far more enjoyable, she felt, than the ice cream socials and book fairs that the elementary schools frequently hosted. She appreciated the formality of this event and was pleased about the opportunity to celebrate the academic success of the district's students.

The ceremony was also a welcome break from her current project, which involved an analysis of student achievement data disaggregated by subgroups. A strong believer in the power of data to inform practice, Emma had spent long hours over the past few weeks reviewing standardized test scores and grade point averages of district students, then associating these measures with a variety of factors, such as race, ethnicity, socio-economic status, disciplinary reports, special education classification, and teacher assignment. Never one to avoid hard truths, Emma had noticed some interesting and disturbing correlations.

The two revelations that were most disquieting involved race. Although the Warsaw School District was relatively diverse with a student population that was 59% White, 35% Black, and 6% Hispanic, students classified as in need of special education were 78% Black and 15% Hispanic. This seemed to be an impossible juxtaposition of percentages; Emma had been so astonished that she had checked the data four times. Then, after requesting another set of data to ensure source accuracy, she had verified it twice more. The numbers were correct. And something was terribly wrong.

The second revelation did not concern academics, but had to do with discipline. Once again, data indicated wide discrepancies connected with race. In grades 7–12, disciplinary incidents disaggregated by race were disconcerting. More than 75% of the incidents resulting in suspensions involved Black students; just over 20% involved Hispanic students. If these figures were accurate (Emma's administrative assistant had requested new data to verify this today), this meant that less than 5% of major disciplinary infractions were linked to students who, racially, comprised almost 60% of the school population. It seemed inexplicable. And Emma had no viable explanation.

However, she knew that it was important to get a sense of how the school reflected the community, so she planned to check local law enforcement records to see whether they had any data regarding race and arrests.

Tonight's celebration offered exactly the kind of respite and inspiration she needed. Energized by the prospect of interacting with students, parents, and faculty who demonstrated the dedication and inclination to succeed, Emma had written an address designed to congratulate and challenge her audience. She intended to commend the students, their parents, and their teachers, for believing in the power of education. By excelling in scholarship, leadership, service, and character, these students exemplified the kind of citizens that a democracy needed in order to prevail in its mission. In a similar vein, Emma's address challenged students to leave the world – beginning with their classrooms, their school community, and their neighborhoods – a better place than when they had arrived. Whether changes were big or small, everyone's actions could – and did – make a difference.

Emma nodded toward the advisor of the National Honor Society (NHS), who had signaled that she'd be introduced in five minutes. She folded her notes and glanced out toward the audience, taking in the scene. Students, both present NHS members and new inductees, were seated in perfectly straight rows. She smiled to herself, noting their uncharacteristically formal attire. Some of their shirts and blouses had creases signifying that they were newly purchased. Leaning forward in pairs and small groups, they whispered incessantly, avoiding eye contact with their parents. Just past the students, parents sat expectantly, cameras in hand. A few waved tentatively at their nervous teens, none of whom waved back.

Suddenly, Emma gasped. She scanned the crowd, trying to dispel the troubling fact she had just grasped. Row by row, she examined the students – new inductees and existing members, as well as the NHS officers who sat on stage. Next, she searched the crowd, once again inspecting them methodically – one row at a time.

Finally, even though she knew what she would find, being fully aware of the demographic status of her district's faculty, Emma looked at the teachers present. As the advisor finished introducing Emma, she stepped toward the podium. She was momentarily blinded by the stage lights, but even more dazed by her realization. This year's National Honor Society at Warsaw High School would induct students representing almost 30% of its student body: yet every single inductee was White.

WORKS CITED

Barth, R. (2001). Making happen what you believe in. Phi Delta Kappan, *82*(2), 446.

Hirsch, E.D. (1996). The schools we need and why we don't have them. New York: Doubleday.

Northouse, P. G. (2009). Introduction to leadership: Concepts and practice. Los Angeles, CA: Sage Publications.

Robbins, P., & Alvy, H. (2004). The new principal's fieldbook: Strategies for success. Alexandria, VA: Association for Supervision & Curriculum Development.

CHAPTER 3

STANDARD 2: SCHOOL CULTURE

Standard 2: *A school administrator is an educational leader who promotes the success of all students by advocating, nurturing, and sustaining a school culture and instructional program conducive to student learning and professional growth.*

Functions:

A. *Nurture and sustain a culture of collaboration, trust, learning, and high expectations*
B. *Create a comprehensive, rigorous, and coherent curricular program*
C. *Create a personalized and motivating learning environment for students*
D. *Supervise instruction*
E. *Develop assessment and accountability systems to monitor student progress*
F. *Develop the instructional and leadership capacity of staff*
G. *Maximize time spent on quality instruction*
H. *Promote the use of the most effective and appropriate technologies to support teaching and learning*
I. *Monitor and evaluate the impact of the instructional program*

The previous chapter discussed the importance of developing a vision that is a descriptive statement of what the school will look like at a specified time in the future. But the achievement of that vision will not happen unless the culture of the school community accepts, supports, and is driven by that vision.

According to Collins (2001), unsuccessful organizations create bureaucracies that "compensate for incompetence and lack of discipline" (p. 121). He found that successful organizations, on the other hand, have a "culture of discipline" where people "became somewhat extreme in the fulfillment of their responsibilities" to achieve a vision (p. 127).

Sergiovanni (1992) discusses a notion similar to that of Collins, focusing on the idea that successful schools have a culture that is more like a community than a bureaucracy. Central to Sergiovanni's notion of community are the "shared values, purposes, and commitment (that) bond the community" (p. 46).

WHAT IS SCHOOL CULTURE?

The term "culture" has numerous definitions, and many include the notion that culture includes those things that determine behavior and expectations. Schein (1985) refers to culture as a:

…pattern of basic assumptions – invented, discovered, or developed by a given group as it learns to cope with its problems… (that) has worked well enough to be considered valid and, therefore, to be taught to new members as the correct way to perceive, think, and feel in relation to those problems. (p. 9)

Bower (1966) provides a simpler definition, stating that culture is "the way we do things around here" (p. 22). Deal and Peterson (1990) see culture as consisting "of the stable, underlying social meanings that shape beliefs and behavior over time" (p. 7). Implicit in all three definitions is the notion that common beliefs, values, and purposes held by the people within the organization help shape the culture which can, in turn, lead to commitment to the organization's vision.

SCHOOL CULTURE AND STUDENT LEARNING

Owens and Valesky (2011), in referring to a study by Rutter, Maughan, Mortimer, and Ouston (1979), state that "research strongly suggests that organizational culture…is a critical factor in student achievement and behavior" (p. 155). They later reference another study (Moos, 1979) "that strongly supports the mounting evidence in the literature that the learning and development of students are significantly influenced by the characteristics of the organizational culture" (p. 155). More recently, MacNeil and Prater (2009) reported that "strong school cultures have better motivated teachers (and) highly motivated teachers have greater success in terms of student performance and student outcomes" (p. 77).

Related to this idea of whether or not culture affects student learning is the concept of a shared vision. Is there, for example, a vision that sets high standards for what students will know, learn, and be able to do when they graduate? Does the vision emphasize the teachers' role in helping students meet and exceed such standards? If so, then the existence of positive common beliefs, values, and purposes (in other words a strong culture that supports the vision) can lead to school improvement.

DEVELOPING A POSITIVE SCHOOL CULTURE

According to Deal and Peterson (1999), "School culture affects every part of the enterprise from what faculty talk about in the lunch room, to the type of instruction that is valued, to the way professional development is viewed, to the importance of learning for all students" (p. 7). In other words, culture helps to establish what teachers believe and do. Do teachers, for example, believe they can affect student learning regardless of the socio-economic status of the students? Do teachers consistently consider the effects that they can have on student achievement? Do they believe that appropriate formative and summative assessment of student performance can help them become more effective? If the answer to these questions is "no," then it is likely that the school is not performing as well as it could and a cultural shift is needed.

Principals can do little to affect student achievement directly, but a meta-analysis of educational research by Marzano, Waters and McNulty (2005) concluded that an educational "leader (who) fosters shared beliefs and a sense of community and cooperation among staff" (p. 48) can create a positive school culture. Marzano et al. maintain that the following behaviors are associated with the development of a positive culture:

- Promoting cohesion among staff
- Promoting a sense of well-being among staff
- Developing an understanding of the purpose among staff
- Developing a shared vision of what the school could be like. (p. 48)

Reeves (2009) outlines four imperatives for establishing a positive culture:

- *Define what will not change:* i.e., articulate the values, principles, traditions, and relationships that will not be lost.
- *Organizational culture will change with leadership actions:* leaders speak most clearly with their actions. Changes they make in decision rules (who has the authority to make what decisions), the allocation of personal time (meetings accepted and canceled), and in establishing relationships (taking the time to understand the personal stories of colleagues) dramatically change the culture.
- *Use the right tools:* leaders must apply the right combination of change tools, varying their strategies to meet the changing needs of the system.
- *Relentless personal attention and "scut work" by the leader:* although leaders must spend time making speeches and attending board meetings, they should, on occasion, take time to do "scut work" e.g., take a turn as a substitute teacher or spend time with bus drivers (pp. 39–40).

School leaders may not be able to influence student performance directly, but many strategies and behaviors can be employed to help create a positive school culture which, in turn, will enhance students' personal and academic development.

CASE STORY 2T: TEACHER LEADER

Jacklyn Perelli's first meeting as the department chair had been a disaster. It was 4:35 p.m. at Harrison Senior High School and, though it had been over a half hour since the meeting ended and the last department members trickled out of her room, she was still in a state of shock. Jacklyn considered herself to be a realist but, given the reception of her department colleagues to her proposed "Action Plan," she felt like a naïve idealist.

As the newly appointed social studies department chair, she embraced the opportunity to serve with equal amounts of optimism and trepidation. Her optimistic side told her that, as chair, she could begin the process of bringing the seven member department together to form a more cohesive unit. But, of course, that need – to bring the department together – was also the source of her trepidation.

She had always been quite successful at "connecting" with her students but she had very little experience working with colleagues – especially in the capacity of having to direct them to do anything. After nine years as a faculty member at Harrison (it seemed like a lifetime to her), Jacklyn knew her social studies colleagues well; that is to say, she knew that they were an eclectic collection of individuals who could be difficult to work with. As a group, they claimed to be "probably the best social studies department in the state." (How they had arrived at that conclusion was a mystery to Jacklyn, but it was a statement she had heard many times). Over the years, Jacklyn noted that her social studies colleagues were given to self-congratulatory remarks about how only their department maintained school rules and held students accountable.

However, Jacklyn was also aware that, among the four core subject areas, the student failure rate in the social studies department was the highest in the school; instead of being chagrined by this statistic, her department colleagues saw this as a badge of honor. To them, it proved that they truly held their students to a high standard. Jacklyn held a different (albeit unspoken) opinion.

Of the 7 department members, 2 were women: Jacklyn and Joyce Kaur (who had been at Harrison for 29 years). Of the 5 men in the department, 1 was the assistant coach for the varsity football team, another was the union president, and a third was a former high school assistant principal who had decided to return to the classroom after two unsuccessful years as an administrator. (He described those two years as unbearable. "I got tired of chasing kids through parking lots" was his pat response when asked why he had left administration.) A fourth male department member ran a struggling dry cleaning business after school. And the fifth – a man named Carl Duprey – was a former town mayor who still dabbled in local politics.

Yes, an eclectic group.

But Jacklyn was convinced that the department had tremendous potential and she was certain that she could help to realize it. She had the energy and determination – as well as irrepressible optimism. With nine years of teaching experience, she was the least senior member of the department. Though she was 32 years old, her social studies colleagues still considered her "a kid" – if they considered her at all. Over the years, Jacklyn had chosen to "fly under the radar" with her department colleagues, opting to take notes during department meetings rather than make comments. In addition, over the past five years, she'd volunteered to coordinate all state and standardized testing for her colleagues, including scoring and reporting.

To her department members, she was, in a sense, invisible. To her building principal (on whom none of these dynamics was lost), she was a highly valued employee.

Jacklyn was also a solid teacher, by any measure. Her student passing rate for the state's high-stakes tests was the highest in the department and students truly liked her. Jacklyn planned her lessons thoroughly and kept her students active and engaged.

When the former department chair, the amiable Chuck Davis (who was noteworthy for serving as a Civil War re-enactor despite the fact that he refused to teach U.S. History) had retired in July, the department chair position had been posted. Chuck's retirement/resignation had come over the summer and was totally unexpected.

Jacklyn had applied for the position without hesitation. She did not anticipate any competition for the job because her department colleagues over the years openly joked about it being "thankless." After a formal selection process (she was interviewed by the principal, Melanie Martiniak, and the school district's assistant superintendent for curriculum), she had been offered the position.

She later learned that there had been one other internal applicant for the position: the most senior member of the department, Carl Duprey.

"You're still here?" The question came from the principal, Melanie, who appeared suddenly at Jacklyn's door. Deep in thought and immersed in self-pity, Jacklyn jumped at the sound.

"Oh... Melanie...hi," said the startled Jacklyn.

Melanie immediately sensed that something was wrong. "Are you all right?"

"Actually, no, I'm not all right," said Jacklyn, and she gestured toward a pile of papers related to the social studies department meeting. "We had our first department meeting today and I wanted it to be – I don't know – different."

"Let me guess," said Melanie, "it didn't go quite as you'd planned?"

"That would be an understatement." For the next ten minutes, Jacklyn described her first meeting as department chair. She had opened the meeting by distributing sign-up sheets for an array of new working groups: a scheduling committee, a curriculum alignment committee, a test analysis committee, a staff development committee, and a technology committee.

"So, what happened?" asked Melanie.

"Sadly, nothing," said Jacklyn. "With the exception of Joyce, who signed up for the scheduling committee, no one volunteered for anything." Jacklyn gestured toward the empty handouts. "And, to make matters worse, it seemed like everything on the agenda became a point of contention."

Jacklyn handed a copy of the agenda to Melanie who noted the numerous topics, several of which related directly to the new committee structure.

"I wanted to begin a discussion on all these issues," said Jacklyn. "You know, the low passing rate, the fact that we don't use technology in our classrooms, our fragmented curriculum. These are critical issues for our department. Instead of beginning a discussion, I ended up listening to complaints about the kids, the parents, the community, the board of education..."

Jacklyn stared out the window at the now empty parking lot and wondered why she had ever thought she was qualified to be the department chair.

CASE STORY 2B: BUILDING LEADER

Hannah Burst was excited. Her proposal to have her middle school sponsor a summer writing workshop had been accepted. She had been careful to craft the proposal so that the school would, at the very least, break even financially. To achieve this, she established a fee structure which would offset the stipends being paid to cover two staff members. It was only under the "no cost to the district" promise that the proposal had been accepted by the board of education.

The purpose of the workshop, scheduled for mid-August, was to offer students an opportunity to engage with writing in a relaxed environment. The model on which the workshop was based promoted choice, self-expression, and opportunities to write personal narratives; and, it celebrated successes – no matter how small – for every child involved.

In order to reduce the student to teacher ratio, Hannah's proposal included a second staff member and she had invited her colleague, Jill Rudnitski, to join her in the endeavor. As the school year drew to a close, parents began to email both Hannah and Jill inquiring about the writing workshop.

One afternoon, as Hannah was working on final grades, Jill came into her room and slumped into a chair. Hannah noted the body language. "What's wrong, Jill?"

Jill sighed heavily. "I'm worried," she said. "It seems that every single student who is enrolled in our summer workshop is weak academically. And the few who are not weak students are discipline problems."

Hannah was surprised at what appeared to be a harsh criticism of the students. Jill was a compassionate and skilled educator who had spent most of her career working with the most challenging students in the school. Her ability to connect with struggling readers and writers had always been her strength; therefore, to hear the anxiety and defeat in her voice was a bit shocking.

Jill continued her review of various phone and e-mail communications with parents: "One mom said her son would 'reluctantly love' coming to writing class. 'Reluctant' is probably the only truth in that line! And I see that Jesse Watkins is enrolled. I just had him in my 7th grade English class this year. He didn't write anything – not a thing – for me the whole school year. Oh, and you'll love this bit of information: Shakatta Ahrens is also in the summer program. She can't stay in a seat long enough to write a single sentence. I'm just afraid that we won't get anything accomplished this summer because we'll be spending all of our time babysitting kids who don't want to be here."

Hannah, who had been teaching for nearly 30 years, waited until she was certain that Jill had exhausted her list of problem students.

"I think you might be overreacting," she said. "We're not promising the world here. It's a four-day workshop. As long as we set the right expectations, I think we'll be okay. Why don't you email the parents and remind them that this is not a remedial class and that the expectation is that students who attend will be asked to write every day. Any deviation from this – including behavior issues – and their child will be asked to leave without a refund. I know that sounds harsh, but if the parents know the summer guidelines, none of this should be a surprise to them."

Hannah knew they should expect some lower achieving and less motivated students in this type of program, but in a room with twenty students and two teachers, she was certain that they would be able to move everyone forward – at least a little. Hannah decided to structure the lessons to make writing fun and interactive. Surely that would appeal to students who did not function well in a more traditional environment. She had watched this model work with other low-performing students and was confident that they could employ strategies that would be equally effective. Besides, a behavior contract was part of the application. Teachers reserved the right to dismiss a student from the class if she or he was disruptive or uncooperative.

But Jill was not placated. "Do you know how many meetings I've already had with these families? Look, I know these parents. I know these kids. They will not do the work and the parents will not support us. With only four days, the program will be a failure before it even gets off the ground."

Jill stood and put her hands on her hips. "You know what, Hannah? I'm out. If these are the kinds of kids we will have in the program, I quit. This is not the way I want to usher in a new school year."

Now it was Hannah's turn. "Jill, come on. Think about what you're saying. We can do this; I know we can."

"Well," said Jill, "you'll have to do it yourself – or get someone else to help you – because I'm out." With that statement, Jill turned and left the room.

In her mind, Hannah ran through the conversation over and over. She respected Jill and truly understood her main point: if students with behavior and motivation problems were enrolled in the summer writing program, it could spoil the environment for everyone. If Jill said these students would be difficult to control, they probably would be. These were not comments Jill would make lightly, and her willingness to bow out left Hannah shaken.

She took out the folder that held the applications and reviewed the roster. Several students were already strong writers who had a passion for the craft. There were also a couple of students who would have to work hard, but they were motivated and would be an asset to the program. The problem was that without the potentially troublesome students Jill had referred to, the program would be too small to break even. Furthermore, Hannah knew that some parents had signed up their children because they expected Jill to be the teacher.

Unsure about how to proceed, Hannah took the problem to the middle school principal, Suzanne Baxter. Suzanne was familiar with the program and had enthusiastically endorsed the original proposal. She was a former English teacher who understood the value of writing, and was a proponent of the dual concepts of "learning to write" as well as "writing to learn." Additionally, since there had been a summer mathematics workshop at the school, she felt the addition of a similar writing workshop was long overdue.

Suzanne listened to Hannah's presentation of the issue, including her concern that Jill's assessment of some of the enrollees was probably accurate. As the building principal, Suzanne was familiar with the students in question, and she agreed that they would pose a significant challenge to the program. But she also shared Hannah's passion for the workshop and her desire to have sufficient enrollment to make it feasible.

Without enough students, the program would not be allowed to run. While Suzanne empathized with the difficulty the current enrollees would pose and did not want this workshop to cause additional stress to the teachers, she also felt an obligation to offer the program to all students.

Finally, Hannah's voice brought Suzanne back from her deliberations. "Suzanne, this program has to run! How can we make Jill understand?"

CASE STORY 2D: DISTRICT LEADER

Bill Adams loved a challenge – and he was ready for a new one.

He had been the principal of tiny Greenbrier Senior High School for nearly a decade. There, he'd developed a reputation as a tech-savvy administrator, using his considerable talents to "map" curricula, analyze test data, and align staff development vertically and horizontally. As a result, Greenbrier, listed in the state's "Small Schools" category, recently had been ranked among the "Top Ten" high schools. Bill was the type of principal who was not only skilled at working with students, parents and teachers; he was also incredibly proficient in curriculum development.

Although satisfied in his current position, when the Director of Curriculum vacancy in the prestigious Strikerville Central School District was posted, Bill was intrigued. He knew that pursuing this position represented a leap of sorts.

If selected, he would be going from a building to a district level position. Also, Bill was aware that Strikerville was a much larger district. When Bill checked the Strikerville Central website, he saw that the high school housed 1,558 students. Greenbrier High School had barely 400. In fact, Strikerville Middle School alone had 824 students – more than double the number of students in Bill's building. Then, there was the issue of Strikerville's four elementary schools. At Greenbrier, there was only one K-8 feeder school preparing students for high school. At Strikerville, there were four large elementary schools.

But the challenge was appealing, so Bill decided to apply. Given his lack of direct experience in a central office setting, Bill was pleasantly surprised to be invited to interview for the position.

During his preparation for the interview, Bill scoured the District's website for information on curriculum maps, textbooks, and common assessments. His research revealed general statements about the K-12 program. However, other than a link to the state's education department website, no data was provided about student performance on the state's high stakes tests.

Bill's initial interview went well. The interview team consisted of teacher representatives from each building, the middle school principal, the special education director, and a parent. The members were impressed by Bill's demeanor, his enthusiasm, and, most importantly, his ability to articulate how technology could address curricular alignment and student assessment. The team recommended Bill "unanimously and enthusiastically" to the superintendent as one of three finalists.

When Bill appeared in the Strikerville Board Room for his second round of interviews, he was greeted by the superintendent and the seven-member board of education. In many ways, Bill found this second interview relatively easy compared to the first round. Most board members' questions centered on relationships: how he might build a team, motivate employees, and deal with difficult people. But after he'd addressed these issues, it was Board member Michelle Binner's turn.

Michelle Binner, in her first year as a board member, was an attorney in a large law firm in the city. She had campaigned on an "Improve Our Schools" platform. Of the 77 school districts in the western part of the state, Strikerville was rated 5th by a regional business newspaper. For board candidate Michelle Binner, this ranking was not acceptable. She felt certain that, given the socio-economic status of the district, its tax base, and its budget, the district's ranking should be higher. Apparently, this message had resonated with district residents because Michelle Binner had won the board seat in a landslide victory.

When it was her turn to address Bill, Michelle did not pose a question. Instead, she directed everyone's attention to the screen behind the board's table. After a few keystrokes on her laptop, a detailed spreadsheet featuring information about area elementary schools appeared on the screen.

"Mr. Adams," she said, "I'd like you to take a few minutes to review this information and provide us with your professional opinion." She handed him the remote.

Bill looked at the screen carefully, scrolling back and forth through several slides. He noted that out of over 200 elementary schools in the region, 3 of the 4 in the Strikerville Central School District – Hunter Elementary, Utica Elementary, and Clarkson Elementary – were ranked 2nd, 4th, and 9th, respectively. Emerson, Strikerville's fourth elementary school, was ranked 55th.

After what seemed like a very long minute, Michelle said, "So, tell us what you think is wrong with this picture."

"Well," said Bill, "honestly, I can't speak specifically about what is wrong, but, clearly something is going on in your elementary schools. The disparity is stunning."

Bill continued. "As you are all certainly aware, there are many, many factors that affect student achievement."

He proceeded to give the board examples of how he had facilitated the process of auditing curriculum, assessments and staff development in his current school and how this process had resulted in increased student performance on state assessments. But everything he said came across as conceptual or procedural, and Bill could sense that he was losing his audience. Even Michelle seemed a bit bored by his rambling response.

"Look," said Bill, "I know that this may not be the most exciting topic in the world. If you're looking for me to recommend a new program or suggest some grand strategy to fix this problem, you're going to be disappointed."

Bill's sudden burst of candor and passion drew his audience back in.

"What I'm talking about is continuous improvement. It is not impossible. It is attainable, but it is time-consuming and it requires teams of teachers and administrators working together – along with the judicious application of technology – to identify our problems and systematically address them. And all of that requires strong leadership that I feel I can provide."

The interview ended strongly. After a brief caucus, the board and the superintendent unanimously agreed that Bill Adams would make an excellent Director of Curriculum.

In the days that followed, Bill experienced the whirlwind of activities that accompanies a change in employment: a job offer was made, and then accepted; a contract was agreed upon. The appointment was formally approved by the board. Finally, Bill submitted a letter of resignation to his employer, and a period of transition began.

As part of the transition plan, Bill used his remaining vacation days to meet with his new superintendent and central office colleagues (including the person he was going to replace, the soon-to-be retiring Susan Barnes), and arrange visits to each of the six Strikerville schools.

Keeping in mind the low ranking of Emerson Elementary School, Bill decided to schedule his first elementary visit with Emerson's principal, Eric Kraus. The phone conversation was brief but pleasant and the two men agreed that Bill would visit Emerson the following Tuesday morning. The plan was to come early to attend a school-wide assembly. That would be followed by a tour of the building.

Bill decided to prepare for each school visit by reviewing student demographic data, class sizes, staffing, teacher turnover rates, and student performance on the state's standardized tests. In his review of Emerson Elementary, Bill noted that Eric Kraus was the most senior of the school principals and that the median age of the faculty in his building was the highest in the district. Another percentage jumped out at him: Emerson had, by far, the highest percentage of students participating in the federal "Free and Reduced Lunch" program – 31%.

As part of his preparation, Bill also had a lengthy discussion with Susan Barnes. "I'm going to Emerson next Tuesday," said Bill. "Is there anything I need to know about Eric Kraus and the faculty before I walk in the door?"

Susan came right to the point. "It's certainly on the board's 'hit list.' It especially caught the eye of board member Binner whose has two children attending that school," she added. She said that in her opinion, and in the opinion of the superintendent, Emerson had the reputation of being the "feel good" school of the district.

"What do you mean by 'feel good'?" asked Bill.

Susan began thoughtfully. "Look, the test scores at Emerson are abysmal…in virtually all subject areas. And the problem is not the lack of a written curriculum; we have a comprehensive curriculum right here." She gestured to a wall full of binders with labels noting subject areas and grade levels. "And the teachers did a great job developing an integrated language arts program."

"So, what's the problem?"

"The problem is time. Our elementary language arts curriculum is designed to be taught in blocks and, unfortunately," said Susan, "each principal is at liberty to create his or her own building schedule. For years now, Eric has devoted two periods per week – that's nearly two hours – to school assemblies. That's two hours of instructional time lost each week. No other principal does that."

Susan seemed frustrated – and exhausted – by her own explanation.

She suggested that if Bill truly wanted to understand the disparity in English language arts (ELA) performance, he should compare the amount of time Emerson teachers and students spent on school-wide assemblies to the time they spent in structured literacy blocks.

In the days leading up to his visit to Emerson, Bill's thoughts were dominated by the concept of "time on task." The idea of a "literacy block" – an extended period of uninterrupted focus on literacy activities – was foreign to him. His administrative experiences were limited to the high school level and had never required him to grapple with flexibility in scheduling. At the high school, there were periods of instruction – each running for 46 minutes. The idea of disciplines competing for time, therefore, was an unfamiliar issue.

On Tuesday morning, Bill found himself sitting in a chair outside Eric Kraus's office. He watched as the usual morning activities of a school unfolded: phones ringing, teachers at the copy machine, P.A. announcements, and staff members streaming in and out of the principal's office.

Eric finally emerged from his office and greeted Bill. The principal was a tall, slender man with thick grey hair. He welcomed Bill warmly and the two exchanged pleasantries. He then led Bill to the school auditorium where the twice-weekly assembly was about to begin.

For the next hour, Bill witnessed the most incredible student-led assembly he had ever seen. Students from all grade levels performed skits, read poetry, and sang songs. He could not help noticing how engaged the students were and how much fun they were having.

After the assembly, Eric gave Bill a tour of the building and then invited him to talk in Eric's office.

"Well," said Bill, "that was an amazing assembly. The level of student engagement was just remarkable."

Eric noted that in recent years, the assemblies had been "targeted for elimination" in light of what he called the district's "obsession with standardized test scores."

"But I promised my faculty, parents, and students that, as long as I'm the principal, those assemblies will be a part of our curriculum," said Eric.

To Bill, the statement seemed to represent a pledge as well as a challenge; and he couldn't resist pushing back.

"Eric, the assemblies are great – no doubt about that. But don't the assemblies cut into time that might be used for a literacy block – where students can immerse themselves in language arts activities?"

"They *are* immersed in language arts activities," said Eric. He seemed ready for the critique.

"You just witnessed nearly an hour of the application of authentic language arts skills," Eric continued. "Where do you think these kids wrote and rehearsed their presentations? They did it in the classroom – and the assemblies allow them to showcase their skills. Sure, our standardized test scores are poor; but I would argue, Mr. Adams, that those scores would be much worse if we cancelled those assemblies and went into test-prep mode. I refuse to do that."

Bill nodded his head thoughtfully. This was not the time to engage in a philosophical discussion about language arts instruction. The issues were too big: standardized testing versus authentic assessment, differentiation versus standardization, increasing test scores versus educating the "whole child."

Bill was a guest in Eric's building so he thanked him for his time and left. As he drove away, Bill recalled the bookshelves of binders filled with curriculum materials lining Susan Barnes' office. He sighed, sure of only one thing: curriculum alignment was much easier to achieve on paper than in reality.

WORKS CITED

Bower, M. (1996). Will to manage. New York: McGraw-Hill.

Collin, J. (2001). Good to great. New York: HarperCollins.

Deal T. E. & Peterson, K. D. (1999). Shaping school culture-the heart of school leadership. San Francisco: Jossey-Bass.

Deal T. E. & Peterson, K. D. (1990). Shaping school culture-Pitfalls, paradoxes, and promises. San Francisco: Jossey-Bass.

Hirsch, E. (1996). The schools we need and why we don't have them. New York: Doubleday.

MacNeil, A. J., Prater, D. L, & Busch, S. (2009). The effects of school culture and climate on student achievement. International journal leadership in education, 12(1), 73–84.

Marzano, R. J., Waters, T, & McNulty, B. A. (2005). School leadership that works: From research to results. Alexandria, VA: ASCD.

Owens, R. G. & Valesky, T. C. (2011). Organizational behavior in education: Leadership and school reform. Upper Saddle River, NJ: Pearson.

Reeves, D. (2009). Leading change in your school. Alexandria, VA: ASCD.

Rutter, M. Maughan, B. Mortimore, P. & Ouston, J. (1979). Fifteen thousand hours: Secondary schools and their effects on children. Cambridge, MA: Harvard University Press.

Schein, E. H. (1985). Organizational culture and leadership. San Francisco: Jossey-Bass.

Sergiovanni, T. (1992). Moral Leadership: Getting to the heart of school improvement. San Francisco: Jossey-Bass.

STANDARD 3: MANAGEMENT OF ORGANIZATION, OPERATIONS, AND RESOURCES

Standard 3: A school administrator is an educational leader who promotes the success of all students by ensuring management of the organization, operations, and resources for a safe, efficient, and effective learning environment.

Functions:

A. *Monitor and evaluate the management and operational systems*
B. *Obtain, allocate, align, and efficiently utilize human, fiscal, and technological resources*
C. *Promote and protect the welfare and safety of students and staff*
D. *Develop the capacity for distributed leadership*
E. *Ensure teacher and organizational time is focused to support quality instruction and student learning*

While a collective vision and supportive culture are essential components of a healthy, high-achieving school, they need to be sustained through appropriate management practices. For building and district leaders, three areas of management stand out as having the greatest impact on the learning environment:

- Student safety
- School finance
- Human resources.

Other aspects of the organization, such as buildings, equipment, data, and time, also need to be managed effectively, but the effective management of the areas above helps to lay a solid foundation for planning and implementing a strong instructional program.

CREATING A SAFE AND SUPPORTIVE LEARNING ENVIRONMENT

Teachers cannot teach and students cannot learn unless they feel safe. Schools that are plagued by bullying and harassment do not make people feel safe and, predictably, student achievement suffers. Citing studies by Pearson, Muller and Wilkinson (2007) and the National School Climate Survey from the Gay, Lesbian and Straight Education Network (2008), the California Safe Schools Coalition reported "that school safety is an important factor in academic success" (Clark & Russell, 2009, p. 1).

Many states and school districts are adopting laws and policies aimed at providing a safe, supportive learning environment. In New York, The Dignity for All Students Act, which took effect in 2012, "…seeks to provide the State's public elementary and secondary school students with a safe and supportive environment free from discrimination, intimidation, taunting, harassment, and bullying" (New York State Education Department, 2010, n.p.).

It is important to note that it is the responsibility of the school leader to *implement* such laws and policies in order to provide students and teachers with a safe and supportive learning environment.

DECLINING FINANCIAL SUPPORT FOR SCHOOLS

Any dip in the economy places tremendous stress on publicly funded organizations – federal, state and local. Over the last few years, this stress has been deeply felt in public school districts. According to a study published by The Center for Public Education, "…rising costs, coupled with no substantial increase in local and state funds, will challenge districts as never before" (Hull, 2010, n.p.).

In order to cope with this crisis, which is expected to continue at some level for some time, school leaders find themselves having to make choices they would not have considered just a few years ago. Should they increase class sizes? Cut funding for sports and music? Eliminate non-mandated subjects and courses? Stop all field trips? Lock the doors of the building as soon as students leave, denying the community access to school buildings and facilities? Eliminate preschool and full day kindergarten? School leaders should answer these questions by making recommendations that most closely align with the school's vision.

According to Guthrie, Hart, Roy, Candoli, and Hack (2008), this will require "…an orientation toward outcomes rather than processes" (p. 47). What is the vision for the school and how can its leaders align financial resources to achieve this vision? At the very least, answering this question involves establishing explicit strategic goals tied to the vision. It will also require school leaders to do what Reeves (2009) refers to as *pulling the weeds*. From a financial point of view, this means reducing or eliminating funding for things that are not aligned with the school's vision.

ALIGNING HUMAN RESOURCES WITH THE SCHOOL'S MISSION AND VISION

Many researchers report a direct relationship between teacher effectiveness and student achievement (Sanders & Rivers, 1996; Darling-Hammond & Young, 2002; Odden, Borman, & Fermanich, 2004). Therefore, hiring and retaining effective teachers are critical steps for implementing a vision for school improvement. These steps are also crucial in establishing and maintaining a student-centered school culture where the needs of students, and not the adults who serve them, shape peoples' beliefs, attitudes, values, and behaviors. Collins (2001) refers to this management practice as *getting the right people on the bus*. He also discusses the difficulty of getting the wrong people off the bus once they are granted tenure

(Collins, 2005). In his view, the probationary period should be a continuation of the selection process rather than an almost certain path to tenure.

In addition to developing practices to ensure that a school has selected and retained strong teachers (and administrators), the allocation of existing human resources must be aligned with the school's vision. This involves making decisions based on the research about student achievement. Leithwood, Seashore-Lewis, Anderson and Wahlstrom (2004) cite a number of variables that can influence student learning, including: allocation of teacher time, teacher working conditions, class size, teaching loads, and teaching in formal areas of preparation. Under the best circumstances, each of these variables will be managed in ways that support the school's vision.

Finally, there is the issue of employee compensation. Typically, about 75% of a school district's budget is spent on employee compensation. Therefore, there are two ways to control costs – manipulate the *level of compensation* paid to employees and/or change *the number of employees* employed by the organization. Wise educational leaders must tailor their compensation practices to the organization's mission and vision while, at the same time, staying within their budgets. From a strategic perspective, compensation practices should be used to attract, retain, and reward personnel. Compensation policies and procedures not aligned with this strategy may be harmful to the culture and make it more difficult to achieve the vision.

In summary, effective management practices are needed in order to sustain the culture and achieve the vision. While there are other parts of the organization that require the leader's attention, a safe learning environment, school finance, and human resources are, arguably, indispensable in the establishment of a solid foundation for school improvement and student success.

CASE STORY 3T: TEACHER LEADER

"Just a second!" Heeding the plea, Marinella Park stopped, her hand on the office door handle. Hiding her impatience, she turned and smiled expectantly at Sandra Rubenstein, the principal's secretary. Although she liked Sandra, Marinella had learned to associate Sandra's presence – and now, apparently, even her voice – with additional work.

"I almost forgot to give you this." Sandra waved a sheaf of papers and gestured for Marinella to take them. "I haven't had a chance to create an electronic version yet, so these are still just photocopies. Remember, they're due by the first of the month – just two weeks from now."

Her apprehensions fulfilled, Marinella took the paper and thanked Sandra for the reminder.

The documents appeared deceptively simple. Each page contained an empty table representing a weekly school schedule. The problem was that Marinella, as social studies department chairperson, was responsible for filling them in – one for every member of the department.

Although Marinella had been a social studies teacher at Clinton High School for twelve years, this was her first year as department chair. And, since the current schedule had been developed by her predecessor, Brian Welker, this was the first time she was responsible for scheduling. Although she dreaded the task, she had to acknowledge a twinge of excitement about the possibility it presented. Brian had maintained tight control of the scheduling process, sharing schedules with teachers in the department only when they were complete and had been already submitted to the principal, making changes by teachers impossible. In fact, Marinella had been elected department chair, in part, because junior faculty members wanted a voice in the creation of their schedules.

Before accepting the position (which had been a result of a very close election; a difference of only one vote had separated Marinella from Brian), Marinella had asked department chairs of other departments how their teacher schedules were determined. Several options had emerged: The science department was simplest, since courses taught were determined primarily by areas of certification (for example, some teachers were certified in biology, others in chemistry or physics). Her colleagues in math drew names each year to create a ranking system; they then selected courses based on those rankings. The English department embraced a specialization model. Each English teacher had chosen a grade level to focus on, and because they all seemed content with this approach, scheduling for them was straightforward.

The social studies department's scheduling process, on the other hand, was complicated – and contentious.

The first problem was the range of courses. Grades 9 and 10 involved global history. No one in the department had concentrated on world history in college, so these courses were unpopular, to say the least. Over the past several years – for as long as Marinella could remember – the courses had been taught by the least senior faculty in the department. Grade 11 social studies concentrated on United States history. Teachers sought to teach U.S. history for three reasons. First, they enjoyed – and were knowledgeable about – the content. Second, students were much more familiar with U.S. history than they were with global history. And third, students in grade 11 were more dedicated, mature, and engaged than students in grades 9 and 10 (partly because mandatory attendance ended after grade 10). These factors were especially relevant now, since student examination scores were being used to evaluate teachers. Global exam results were significantly lower than U.S. history exam results.

While the distribution of core courses in social studies teachers' schedules was always challenging, the distribution of electives was even worse. Here, the conflict between specialization and flexibility was particularly forceful. Several factors contributed to the discord regarding department electives. Many of the veteran teachers had developed the electives and worked to ensure their adoption decades earlier. Therefore, they felt entitled to teach them. Brian, for example, had taught every section of sociology since the course had been first offered twenty years ago. Of course, his experience contributed to his effectiveness, but newer teachers argued that they should be allowed to teach it, as well – especially Abbey Robbins, who had minored in sociology in college. When Abbey had asked, at a department meeting last spring, about teaching the course, Brian had instead offered her psychology, an elective that was available because of a faculty member's retirement.

The specialization/flexibility debate was ongoing, but had always occurred behind the scenes. Marinella had heard arguments on both sides. Certainly, the advantages of having a teacher with experience and expertise in a particular content area were clear. However, the notion that a certain teacher "owned" a course seemed unfair and even anti-intellectual. Marinella, herself, believed that teaching new courses enhanced her professionalism; both content knowledge and pedagogical practices were strengthened. In addition, having teachers who could teach a wide range of courses made the scheduling process infinitely easier. For example, two sections of a course could run simultaneously if two different teachers were assigned to them. The current system required gyrations that, at times, seemed to require superhuman managerial skills. Greater flexibility would streamline the process for both Marinella and her principal.

"Hey...our fearless leader!"

Marinella was jolted from her thoughts by Abbey's voice. She smiled at her young colleague.

"Are those what I think they are?" Abbey looked at the scheduling sheets Marinella was holding. "I can't wait to see how regime change affects our schedules!" She nudged Marinella with her elbow and lowered her voice. "I know it's going to be tough, but we're behind you all the way. See you later!"

As Marinella watched Abbey walk toward her classroom, the reality of her parting words sunk in; the monthly department meeting was this afternoon. She would have to prepare a plan, some kind of process, to assign her colleagues to courses for next fall. They were expecting a participatory approach. And the more she pondered it, the more appealing Brian's private process seemed.

CASE STORY 3B: BUILDING LEADER

Drew Sutton was moving up rapidly as a school administrator. Four years ago, he had been a biology teacher at Grant Senior High School. Then, just a few weeks after receiving his administrator's certificate, the assistant principal at Drew's high school had been involved in a serious auto accident and was forced to take a leave of absence to undergo extended rehabilitation. The Grant Senior High School principal, Marie Randazzo (with whom Drew had worked closely and productively during his administrative internship), had offered Drew the temporary position of assistant principal.

Drew's six month tenure in this position was nothing less than a colossal success. He was a natural in every respect. His strong science background manifested itself in decisions that were logical, rational, and devoid of emotion. Teachers loved him because he promptly responded to their student discipline concerns and he always followed through with them, so they had a strong sense that they were being heard and, more importantly, that things were getting done.

The students took to Drew, too. It certainly helped that he had been a popular and effective biology teacher in that building, but Drew seemed to form instant connections with just about every student, even those who hadn't known him through classroom interactions. Between periods, students were often seen talking to – and good-naturedly kidding with – the man they affectionately called "Mr. S."

Drew felt strongly that the time between periods was crucial to maintaining an orderly environment, so he worked with the staff and requested that each teacher stand (and be visible) at his or her classroom door during the four minutes between classes so that, as Drew said, "there would be a strong adult presence in the corridors."

"When I walk down a hallway between classes," Drew said at a recent faculty meeting, "I want to see a wall of teachers. It's hard for kids to misbehave when there are so many adults standing around watching them."

"Plus," added Drew, "this will move the kids along – and the odds of a student coming late to one of your classes will be just about zero."

The idea was simple, logical, and brilliant. The staff bought into the idea and Drew's reputation as a highly competent administrator was solidified. Marie Randazzo was, perhaps, the happiest person in the school. She had discovered an administrative gem.

Drew never returned to the classroom as a teacher. In fact, after the school year ended, he did not return to Grant Senior High School. He applied for several secondary level principal positions in the area and, given his credentials, references, experiences, and successes, he landed one in the Batavia City School District.

Batavia Senior High School posed a real challenge for a veteran administrator, let alone a novice like Drew. But he had inherited two strong assistant principals and, applying the same methods and strategies that had worked so well at Grant, he began to turn around this urban, working class school. Drew accomplished this by, in a sense, intensifying the concept of "adult presence."

One of his central strategies involved engaging with the local police department and coordinating a program that included "police liaisons" – officers who were specially trained and who exhibited the proper dispositions to walk the corridors of the school and interact with students on a regular basis. It was Drew's "wall of teachers" writ large: in addition to teachers monitoring the corridors, police officers would, as well. Three days per week – every Monday, Wednesday, and Friday – a Batavia City Police car was parked conspicuously in front of the senior high school, sending the message that this was a place of order and discipline.

The program seemed effective. At the end of Drew's first full year as principal, the number of fights and altercations was reduced by nearly 70%. Suspensions were down from 476 total days to 189. Even the level of overall cleanliness in the building improved. Custodians noted that there was considerably less litter in the corridors and that vandalism had virtually disappeared. Drew's superintendent was thrilled with the performance of his new principal. The school was finally under control.

At the end of the school year, Drew received a special commendation from the Batavia Central School District's Parent Teacher Association (PTA) Executive Committee. The plaque cited him for his "Dedication to the students and contributions to the Batavia community."

His accomplishments were noticed by the broader educational community, as well. After three years at Batavia Senior High School, Drew was recruited by Dr. David Cooper, the superintendent of the Fox Valley Central School District, to serve as the principal of Heritage Heights Senior High School.

Fox Valley was a relatively new but fast growing outer suburban community. It was, in many ways, the antithesis of the city of Batavia. The five-year-old Heritage Heights High School complex was an architectural dream, with a huge three-story glass-enclosed foyer, three full-size gymnasiums, two swimming pools, and a field house with artificial turf which provided an indoor practice site for the football, baseball, softball, soccer and lacrosse teams.

Drew couldn't resist the opportunity to serve as an educational leader in an upper middle-class community. He couldn't believe that just three years earlier he had been laboring with 10th graders in a biology lab. Now, he was the principal of one of the largest and most prestigious high schools in the region.

But he had been recruited for a reason. During the interview process and during the appointment phase, David Cooper had explained to Drew that all was not well with Heritage Heights. The beautiful building and incredible amenities, he noted, masked a building whose students had mediocre standardized test scores, unacceptably high rates of suspensions, and an average daily attendance rate of only 89%. These problems were certainly not as severe as those of working-class schools such as Grant or Batavia, but they were unacceptably high for a community like Fox Valley.

Drew embraced the new challenge and put into place the strategies he had used so effectively in other settings. After a month of school, Drew was dismayed to see students still milling around in the corridors well after the bell. Though Drew attempted to persuade the faculty to be visible at their doorways, their response was half-hearted. He found himself walking from door to door between periods reminding teachers about this expectation. No one openly defied him; they simply ignored the mandate when he was not around.

The congested unsupervised corridors, as they always do, led to students' coming late to class. That led to an increase in detentions. The crowded conditions gave rise to pushing and shoving. A few fights broke out and several students were suspended.

By mid-October, Drew had decided to take a firmer stand in building. He contacted the Fox Valley Police Department and asked whether they had liaison program like the one that had been so successful in Batavia. Though not identical to the Batavia program, he learned that the Fox Valley Police Department did have something called a "community outreach" officer. Drew arranged a meeting with the officer in charge.

The next morning, at about 9:00 a.m. – well into the second period – Drew met with Officer Ron Timmons. As the two men discussed ways to create a "police presence" in the building, Drew was interrupted by his secretary.

"Mr. Sutton, Superintendent Cooper is on the phone and he said he would like to speak with you."

"Sure," said Drew, "put him through."

"Do you want me to step out?" asked Officer Timmons, rising from his chair.

"No, no – stay right here. It shouldn't take long." Drew gestured to Officer Timmons to remain seated.

The phone buzzed and Drew picked it up. "Good morning, Dr. Cooper. What can I do for you?"

"Well," the superintendent replied, "the first thing you can do is get that goddamned police car off our property."

Drew was stunned. He swallowed, then replied, "What's the problem, Dr. Cooper?"

"The *problem*," snapped the superintendent, "is that our community equates police presence with trouble, and I don't want our parents to think that their school is so out of control that we have to bring in the cops. Now get that car off our premises…now!"

Drew knew from the click on the line that the superintendent hadn't waited for his response. Officer Timmons *was* waiting, however, and Drew knew a quick decision was needed.

He just wasn't sure what that decision should be.

CASE STORY 3D: DISTRICT LEADER

Pineville, a school district located in the rural northwest, had just over 2,000 students attending two K-8 schools and one high school. Although the total student population remained steady over the years, the percentage of district students who qualified for the federal "Free and Reduced Lunch" program had increased from 15% to 27% over the last six years.

In addition, a significant number of students who came from low income households were also classified as ELLs – English Language Learners – indicating that English was not their first language. These changes in student demographics were felt district wide, resulting in resources being allocated for additional teachers for the English as a Second Language (ESL) program.

Dr. Angela Skally was in her sixth year as the assistant superintendent for instruction and human resources. She had previously served as a principal in a nearby school district. Prior to becoming a school administrator, Angela had taught music for twelve years.

Pineville was recognized as a good, but not outstanding, school district. Typically, 70 to 75% of a Pineville High School graduating class went on to college; but a closer look at the numbers indicated that more than half of *that* group attended the nearby community college rather than institutions granting bachelor's degrees. Administrators, school counselors and teachers were surprised – and perplexed – by the fact that no Pineville graduates in recent memory had enrolled in prestigious out-of-state colleges or universities.

In addition, the percentage of students who earned diplomas from Pineville High School within four years, an expectation of the state education department, had dropped from 94% to 81% over the past five years. Unless the school district could increase this percentage, the high school would be classified by the state as a "school in need of improvement" – a designation that required significant internal restructuring.

The image of Pineville as a successful school district was at odds with its standardized test scores which were below the state average. Despite its questionable academic performance, the high school boasted a strong interscholastic athletic program, having won local championships in football, girls' basketball, indoor track, girls' lacrosse and baseball. The school had 22 varsity sports teams with junior varsity and modified programs in most areas. Its marching band had won numerous state and national awards. In fact, the band was scheduled to participate in the Thanksgiving Day Parade in New York City in the fall. The community proudly displayed these various honors on billboards along the major highway that ran through the town. Finally, the district's two K-8 schools were held in high regard by the parents who consistently supported school functions and fundraisers.

Last year, Angela, after lengthy discussions with the superintendent, school board, high school principal, teachers, parents, and community leaders, had developed a comprehensive high school improvement plan. The plan contained specific goal targets: increase the percentage of students who graduate from high school within four years to 90%; increase the percentage of graduates who attend college to 80%; and increase the number of students who attend colleges and universities that are regarded as "prestigious," for example, Ivy League schools, military academies, and highly competitive public colleges as recognized by publications such as *U.S. News and World Report*.

The plan was approved by the board of education, coupled with a promise to allocate additional funding for teachers, equipment, staff development and other resources critical to the success of the plan. The school was given three additional teachers to provide support for the plan, bringing the total number of teachers at the high school to 47. Additional resources were promised for the following year.

Around mid-February, Angela attended the first of two monthly board of education meetings. Budget discussions, which began in December, were always driven by changes in state funding for schools. If state funding was increased, programs were almost assured of being retained; if funding was reduced, staff and program cuts were inevitable.

At this February meeting, Angela learned that news from the state capital was not good; funding would be "frozen" at the previous year's level. The local paper noted that the combination of an anti-tax movement and a new law limiting property tax increases, along with the funding "freeze," represented the "perfect storm."

With rising costs for salaries, health insurance, employee pensions, and utilities, Pineville was faced with a $2 million shortfall. The board, working with the superintendent, had agreed in December to find ways to close the gap. In January, the board adopted the following cost saving measures:

- place a moratorium on any new programs
- discontinue membership in the state and national school boards associations
- reduce the number of late afternoon bus runs
- eliminate field trips
- reduce funding for supplies and equipment by 20%
- reduce spending on programs for students with disabilities by providing programs within, rather than outside, the district.

In the words of a local reporter (who apparently couldn't resist an old metaphor), the board had eliminated the "low hanging fruit." Despite the cliché, the point was made: Those cuts had reduced the gap between revenues and expenses by only $300,000; they were essentially painless and non-controversial – and they certainly would not affect any academic area.

The board of education meeting began the same way board meetings always began at Pineville, with the recognition of students followed by an opportunity for those in attendance to address the board.

Students from the state championship football and field hockey teams were recognized and the band director provided an update on the school's participation in the Macy's Parade. Several parents then addressed the board, requesting that all sports and music programs be preserved and threatening to campaign against the school budget – which was subject to approval by the residents in May – if funding to these programs was reduced.

They were followed by middle school Spanish and French teachers who urged the board to continue to offer foreign language to all students in grades 5–8 although state education department regulations mandated foreign language instruction only for grades 7 and 8. And, interestingly, the "low hanging fruit" was, perhaps, not low enough because a contingent of nearly 20 parents threatened to sue the district if there were any changes in the special education program.

The board president, Sam Wilton, thanked the community members for their input. Then, he offered a motion: "I move that any employee retiring or resigning from the district not be replaced."

The district superintendent, Dr. Sean Morrissey was stunned. Where had this come from? But before he could respond, the motion was seconded by the vice-president. In quick vote that followed, much to Sean's relief, the motion was defeated 4 to 3. Undeterred, the board president followed that failed vote with another motion: "I move that the board direct the superintendent to present a plan for cutting spending on personnel in all schools by an average of 5% for next year and that this plan be presented at the next board meeting." The motion was again seconded by the vice-president and, with no discussion, passed 4 to 3.

The superintendent, as well as the administrators and teachers present, left the meeting in disbelief, aware that people and programs needed to be cut – but with no clear idea of where to begin.

The following morning, Sean asked Angela to report to his office to discuss budget-related matters.

He began, "Okay Angie, you heard what I heard. The board wants a 5% reduction in personnel for each school in two weeks. Parents have threatened to vote down the budget if we cut funding for sports and the marching band. The middle school foreign language teachers are campaigning against cuts to their program, though I'm not sure we can continue to offer foreign language in fifth and sixth grade. And the parents of our special education students are threatening a lawsuit."

He continued. "By next Tuesday, I need your list of priorities in terms of where we can cut positions, K-12. Other than mandated programs, nothing is off the table. Programs and class sizes must be considered. I think we need a cut greater than five from the high school, so –"

Angela interrupted, "Sean, you and the board agreed to support the high school improvement plan and, without that support, we are at risk of not meeting state mandates for academic performance. If that happens, we will be labeled as a school 'in need of improvement.' In addition to being a 'black eye' for the district, it could jeopardize future state funding."

Sean sat at his desk, rubbing his temples slowly.

Angela wasn't finished. "And we have to do a better job of helping students get ready for college. Cutting resources rather than adding is simply a horrible idea. We'll never meet state mandates even if we *maintain* current spending levels. What do you want me to do?"

In rare display of emotion, Sean responded, "Angie, this school district pays you a very good salary to provide answers – not questions! Get me that list by Tuesday. I want you to identify the priorities and the impacts of 5%, 7% and 9% reductions in staffing costs. Is that clear?"

Dumbfounded and hurt, Angela left the superintendent's office. She tried to get a grip on the conflicting nature of her responsibilities: How was she supposed to craft a plan recommending staff cuts and also meet the district's goals for student achievement?

How did they expect her to do more with less?

WORKS CITED

Clarke, T. J., & Russell, S. T. (2009). School safety and academic achievement. (California Safe Schools Coalition Research Brief No. 7). San Francisco, CA: California Safe Schools Coalition.

Collins, J. (2001). Good to great. New York: HarperCollins.

Collins, J. (2005). Good to great and the social sectors: a monograph to accompany good to great. New York: HarperCollins.

Darling-Hammond, L., & Young, P. (2002). Defining "highly qualified teachers": What does "scientifically based research" actually tell us? Educational Researcher, *31*(9), 13–25.

Guthrie, J.W., Hart, C. C., Ray, J. R., Candoli, I. C., & Hack, W. G. (2008). Modern school business administration: A planning approach. Boston: Pearson.

Hull, J. (2010). Cutting to the bone: How the economic crisis affects schools. Retrieved from http://www.centerforpubliceducation.org.

Kosciw, J. G., Diaz, E. M., & Greytak, E. A. (2008). 2007 National School Climate Survey: The experiences of lesbian, gay, bisexual and transgender youth in our nation's schools. New York: GLSEN.

Leithwood, K., Seashore-Lewis, K., Anderson, S., & Wahlstrom, K. (2004). How leadership influences learning. New York: Wallace Foundation.

Odden, A., Borman, G., & Fermanich, M. (2004). Assessing teacher, classroom, and school effects, including fiscal effects. Peabody Journal of Education, 79(4), 4–32.

Pearson, J., Muller, C., & Wilkinson, L. (2007). Adolescent same-sex attraction and academic outcomes: The role of school attachment and engagement. Social Problems, 54(4), 523–542.

Reeves, D. (2009). Leading change in your school. Alexandria, VA: ASCD.

Sanders, W. L. & Rivers, J. C. (1996). Cumulative and residual effects of teachers on future student achievement. Knoxville, TN: University of Tennessee.

New York State Education Department. (n.d.) The dignity act. Retrieved from http://www.p12.nysed.gov/dignityact.

STANDARD 4: COLLABORATION WITH FAMILIES AND COMMUNITIES

Standard 4: A school administrator is an educational leader who promotes the success of all students by collaborating with families and community members, responding to diverse community interests and needs, and mobilizing community resources.

Functions:

A. *Collect and analyze data and information pertinent to the educational environment*
B. *Promote understanding, appreciation, and use of the community's diverse cultural, social, and intellectual resources*
C. *Build and sustain positive relationships with families and caregivers*
D. *Build and sustain productive relationships with community partners*

A school administrator has responsibilities that go well beyond attending to the needs of students, faculty, and staff. To meet ISLLC Standard 4, a highly competent administrator must also collaborate with families and community members, respond to diverse community interests and needs, and mobilize community resources.

Collaboration poses a unique challenge for school leaders because the power relationship between the school leader and these outside entities (families and community members) is quite different from the one held within the school environment. A superintendent or building principal may have line authority over faculty, but certainly not over parents or community members. This reality makes it necessary for administrators and other school leaders to think about the implications of these relationships in terms of communication, decision-making, and empowerment.

In addition, because these entities are positioned *outside* the school, a school leader – to be successful in meeting Standard 4 – must learn to interact with organizations that often have different structures, values, goals and purposes.

COLLABORATION AND PARTNERSHIPS

Collaboration is defined as "working together toward a common goal or set of goals" (Cowan, Swearer, & Sheridan, 2004, p. 201). The word "partnership" is also connected to the concept of collaboration. Epstein, Sanders, Simon, Salinas,

Jansorn, and Voorhis (2002) have written extensively about the need to develop family-school-community partnerships to improve student achievement. Cowan et al. (2004) differentiate the two:

> A primary difference between home-school collaboration and home-school partnership is that home-school collaboration implies a process related to a specific goal or set of goals that may be relatively short-term...whereas home-school partnership implies a long-term, ever-evolving relationship between parents and members of the school setting extending beyond time-limited problem solving and goal achievement. (p. 202)

Consequently, schools would *collaborate* with parents, for example, to organize a school dance or build a playground but would have to form a *partnership* if they wished to include parents in addressing long-range problems related to attendance, standardized test scores, or parent-teacher communications.

NEEDED: A PARADIGM SHIFT

It is important for school leaders to recognize that the history of parental and community involvement in schools is limited in scope. Until the reauthorization of the Individuals with Disabilities Education Improvement Act (IDEIA) in 1997 and the passage of the "No Child Left Behind Act" in 2001, schools were not compelled by law to involve parents in any form of shared decision-making. This fact is significant because most schools are not (and have never been) *structured* to include parents as co-partners in the education of their children.

In the past, parents have been invited to come to most schools under these limited conditions:

1. The school contacts the home and requests a "parent conference." Implicit in this request is the fact that the student is experiencing academic difficulty or has violated a major school rule (for example, fighting, vandalism, excessive tardiness, or absenteeism).
2. The school sponsors an event and invites parents to attend. Such events would include, for example, the annual parent-teacher conference, a science fair, a sports event, or a concert. Implicit in these invitations is the desire of the school to "showcase" elements of its program.
3. The school issues a request for parent volunteers to assist in any number of traditional capacities such as chaperone for a school dance or field trip, or to assist in a fundraising activity.

Note that in each case, the school initiates the contact and that parents are expected to be informed, to be entertained, or to work. This parent involvement paradigm – typical of what Davies, Henderson, Johnson and Mapp (2006) refer to as "Come-if-We-Call" schools – persists today. The implicit messages being sent to parents include the following: We (the school) have all the answers, we are the experts, and you should appreciate the great job we're doing.

Given the pervasiveness of this model, the school leader who wishes to effect *meaningful* parental involvement must recognize that, as a society, we continue to move from deterministic systems toward purpose-seeking systems. Betts (1992) explains: "In social terms, we are moving from "dictatorial" to "participative" organizational styles. In order to make this kind of transition, it is necessary only to shift perspective from a *one-to-many* toward a *many-to-one* orientation." (p. 39)

Effective school leaders, then, do not see themselves as centers (or singular sources) of information, knowledge and expertise. Instead, they exhibit an understanding of the roles of parents and community members in a professional learning environment.

EMBRACING A PARTNERSHIP PHILOSOPHY

An effective school leader must embrace a partnership philosophy regarding home-school collaboration. This philosophy recognizes that parents are invaluable members of the educational team. However, as with any belief system, it is the school leader's actions that ultimately enhance or inhibit the "operationalizing" of this philosophy, one which must be measured against the reality of the school, itself.

Davies et al. (2006) provide a useful checklist for school leaders who wish to determine the extent to which their schools have the qualities and ingredients necessary to foster true partnerships. The related characteristics, presented along a continuum, include the number and type of interactions between the school and families; social services availability; parental involvement in curriculum development and test analysis; school resources available to parents; the existence and availability of multicultural materials; teacher-parent communication; and power sharing opportunities – among others.

ECOLOGY THEORY AND SYSTEMS THINKING

The process of change in schools is difficult primarily because school leaders lack knowledge and understanding of Ecology Theory which is grounded in Systems Thinking (Senge, 1990). In order to implement a meaningful partnership with parents, school leaders must recognize that an individual's interactions across and within systems are multifaceted and multi-determined over time.

Ecology Theory, based on the work of Bronfrenbrenner (as cited in Cowan, et al., 2004) is concerned with the interaction between an individual and various contextual systems. He cites four such systems:

- The microsystem which is concerned with the individual and his/her immediate environment e.g., the child and the classroom.
- The mesosystem which involves the interrelation between major systems in the individual's life, e.g., the school and the home.
- The exosystem which is concerned with environments not directly related to the individual but still influencing his/her life e.g., a parent's workplace.

- The macrosystem which includes overall cultural or subcultural patterns and influences e.g., federal and state policies and legislation, global economic factors. (p. 203)

An effective school leader recognizes how systems influence, and are influenced by, one another and acknowledges that individuals do not exist in isolation.

For example, Cowan et al. (2004) posit three factors which influence how a family interacts with educators. They list family-related factors (which include the family's history with the school); school-related factors (essentially, the culture of the school – its beliefs, values and expectations); and community factors (the community's own set of norms, values and expectations regarding home-school collaboration).

To underscore the influence of community factors, it might be helpful to consider the perception of law enforcement in general, and the police, in particular. In some communities, a partnership with the police department (which might include police presence on campus) would be considered a sign of safety, order, and control in the school. In other communities, it could be interpreted as the school being out of control and in desperate need of police intervention. Some communities value police presence; others are ambivalent about it.

MEANINGFUL RELATIONSHIPS IN A PROFESSIONAL LEARNING COMMUNITY

Establishing a partnership is a complicated process that cannot be presented as a recipe. Rather, the effective school leader should recognize that a partnership is based on *building relationships*. This process requires time, is based on respect, and it implies that control must be shared.

DuFour and Eaker (1998) elaborate on the six standards for parental involvement developed and adopted by the National Parent Teacher Association. These standards provide a framework for the school leader who values, and wishes to develop, a truly participative school structure. They address issues of communication, parenting, student learning, volunteering, making decisions, and collaborating with the community.

Not surprisingly, they devote a great deal of discussion to the importance of communication which, in many ways, drives the success of the other five standards. The effective school leader, note DuFour and Eaker (1998), understands that communication with parents is regular, two-way, meaningful, and timely.

The key phrases here are "two-way" and "meaningful." The examples of traditional school-parent communications given at the beginning of this chapter are not two-way nor are they necessarily meaningful. School leaders today must provide information to parents and solicit input, feedback, and assistance on a much broader range of issues including program analysis and evaluation, student performance data, state and federal educational policies, student placement options, and parental training opportunities.

Engaging parents in such activities will meet both the letter and spirit of the concept of *meaningful* parental and community involvement.

CASE STORY 4T: TEACHER LEADER

In the best sense of the phrase, Jennie Steltermann felt that she had "seen it all" in her 29 years at Rhinebridge Middle School. She had served under six different principals and eleven assistant principals since her arrival as a very young math teacher nearly three decades ago. She had seen policies and practices come and go. She had witnessed many newly-minted administrators who had arrived at Rhinebridge filled with "vision statements" and "philosophies" and "goals" and "outcomes" only to see them use the school as a stepping stone for better paying positions in more prestigious school districts.

Jennie had, at one time, considered getting her administrative certificate, but the fact was that she loved teaching at Rhinebridge. After completing 14 years as a math instructor, she felt a desire for change and she returned to her local college to become a school counselor. She did not want to lose contact with what had driven her to be an educator in the first place: the students.

When a counseling position opened at Rhinebridge, Jennie applied and was offered the position. This was not unexpected because Jennie was considered to be the cultural center of the school. When first hired, Jennie had been the last of a large wave of new teachers and, as a function of demographics, seemingly overnight (if 29 years can ever be equated to overnight) she found that she was, by far, the most senior faculty member on staff as her older colleagues retired one by one. She also found that, increasingly, administrators and teachers came to her for advice and guidance. Jennie possessed what the literature on organizational development referred to as "institutional memory." She knew every school policy and practice. She knew when they had changed, who had changed them, and why.

As the school counselor, Jennie Steltermann also knew the community well. She had been a district resident for over 20 years and through daily interactions with parents and students, coupled with occasional and unfortunate interactions with the police and social service agencies, she had become familiar with all the characteristics of the Rhinebridge community. She was particularly aware of recent changes. Rhinebridge had never been affluent, but the past decade had taken a toll in terms of the socio-economic status of the town's population. The percentage of students on the federal "Free and Reduced Lunch" program had risen steadily from a modest 16% a decade ago to 59% for the current school year. Jennie was well aware of these statistics because, among her other duties, she was responsible for filing mandated federal reports.

The changes in the community and in the school were not lost on the teaching staff and Jennie noticed that faculty meeting discussions often veered toward criticisms of the community: the lack of parental involvement and support; the poor attendance at Open House; and the plunging standardized test scores. The school personnel seemed disconnected from the community it was supposed to serve.

So when a phone call came from Anita Trujillo, the mother of 8th grader Tomasita Trujillo, Jennie was not surprised.

CHAPTER 5

Mrs. Trujillo came right to the point: "I want you to do something about Mr. Kress, Tomasita's math teacher. Tomasita said that he picks on her every day in class. She said that he threatened her last week; he told her he's going to send her to summer school. And today, he told her to stop looking at Devon."

From years of experience, Jennie knew how to work with parents. She knew how to be respectful, how to acknowledge parental concerns, and how to de-escalate the inevitable emotions that arise when parents believe that their children are being mistreated. Jennie listened as the mother laid out a list of transgressions perpetrated by Mr. Kress and she was profoundly aware that she was getting only one side of the story.

In the course of the conversation, Jennie determined that Mrs. Trujillo needed to speak with Mr. Kress directly, so she scheduled a meeting (tentatively, since she had not confirmed the date and time yet with Mr. Kress) for 3:30 the next day – just after dismissal. The meeting would take place in Jennie's office and would include Mr. Kress, Mrs. Trujillo, and Jennie.

Jennie knew Jonathan Kress well. He had spent his whole career (twelve years) teaching 8th grade math at Rhinebridge Middle School. From Jennie's perspective, Jonathan Kress represented the stereotypical male math teacher; often covered with chalk dust, he seemed to be perpetually in front of the board doing math problems and posing procedural questions to students. He had strong classroom management skills and students seemed to both respect and fear him.

Jennie re-focused her attention on the student in question, Tomasita, and pulled her file. As Jennie recalled, Tomasita seemed like an average 8th grade girl. She exhibited nervous energy and bouts of lethargy, depending on the situation. With her friends and in the school corridors, she was an extrovert: entertaining, funny, and a bit boisterous. In class, she sometimes appeared sullen, withdrawn and non-communicative. Though her grades were decent (generally in the low 80's), the "Teacher Comments" section on her grade 6 and grade 7 report cards featured remarks such as "Needs to be more attentive" and "Needs to participate in class discussions."

Jennie walked from her office to the math wing and found Jonathan in room 232 – at the board. As a former math teacher, she could tell that he was demonstrating how to graph a line from an equation. She heard him use the phrase "linear function." Jennie waved to get his attention.

"Sorry to interrupt," she began.

"No problem, Jennie," he said. "We were just about to begin some group work. What brings you back to the old math wing?"

Jennie remembered when Jonathan was hired over a decade ago. She had been the chair of the interview committee and the group had unanimously recommended him for the position. He had been so young then, and so idealistic. And now, here he was, a father of three whose hair was showing quite a bit of gray.

"I don't want to take up your class time," she said, "but I just got off the phone with Tomasito Trujillo's mother."

Jennie went on to explain the concerns raised by the mother, acknowledging that a meeting with the mother "might be a good idea." She also told Jonathan that she had tentatively scheduled such a meeting with the three of them the next day at 3:30. Jennie noticed that Jonathan remained silent – uncomfortably so – throughout the interaction.

"So, does 3:30 work for you?"

"Sure, 3:30 is fine," replied Jonathan. Then he added, "Jennie, I've got to get back to my class."

The next day – at exactly 3:28 – Jennie was sitting in her office with Mrs. Trujillo (who had shown up 15 minutes early) waiting for Jonathan to arrive. Looking through the glass window of her closed door, Jennie saw Jonathan walk into the office followed by Ralph Lorigo, the head of the math department and Dominic Palumbo, the teachers' union representative.

Jennie was horrified. Why had Jonathan requested their presence at this meeting? Clearly, they were here as a group. Why hadn't he mentioned it to her?

Mrs. Trujillo noticed the change in Jen's demeanor. "Is something wrong?" she asked.

"No, Mrs. Trujillo, there's nothing wrong. Please stay right here. I'll be back in a minute."

CASE STORY 4B: BUILDING LEADER

"Mr. Romero?"

Victor Romero stopped, set his face into what he hoped looked like an authentic smile, and turned to greet the familiar voice. As principal of Westbrook Elementary School, he was busy with mid-summer paperwork: writing end-of-year reports for the superintendent and developing plans for the upcoming school year.

"Mrs. Walters!" Victor replied, holding out his hand to shake hers. "How nice to see you again. I hope you and your family are enjoying the summer break."

"Oh, we certainly are," Jo Ann Walters smiled in return, but her face quickly reverted to its more characteristic purposefulness. "As you may recall, my youngest, Joelle, will be starting kindergarten here in the fall, so we are making the most of these last weeks together. I must admit, though, that I am more nervous than she is, especially since I recently learned about the new teacher selection policy." Jo Ann frowned, making her anxiety and displeasure perfectly visible in her expression.

Victor, briefly considering his options, gestured for her to step into his office. He decided that he might as well deal with this issue immediately, since it was not likely to dissipate in the coming weeks before school began. Mrs. Walters was just the first of many parents he expected to hear from, and he had a feeling that none of them was going to be happy. Her reference to the policy as "teacher selection," rather than what the district called the "student assignment" policy was a revealing shift in terminology, one that clearly illustrated her perspective on the matter.

As Jo Ann sat down across from him, Victor once again pasted on a smile. "So, Mrs. Walters, what exactly have you heard?"

"Well, you know how much I love this school – and how *well* my three older children did here."

Victor nodded, encouraging her to continue.

"I feel certain that part of the reason for their continued academic success is that they had an excellent foundation – starting in kindergarten." She cleared her throat and finished, "Specifically, with Mrs. Brent."

Victor nodded slowly. He knew what was coming next.

"What I've heard lately, Mr. Romero, is that – beginning this year – parents will not be able to request particular teachers for their children. So, naturally, I am worried that Joelle may be the first and only child in our family who won't have the experience of kindergarten with Mrs. Brent. As you know, the projects she does are extraordinary. I know this may sound superficial, but I honestly cannot imagine kindergarten without hatching baby chicks and watching cocoons transform into butterflies. And Joelle has been waiting, practically since birth, to be in Mrs. Brent's kindergarten. She actually remembers coming in with me when I volunteered in her older brother's class. She would be devastated if she were in another teacher's class…truly devastated."

Listening to her extol the virtues of Eleanor Brent, Victor's mind momentarily wandered. He guessed that Mrs. Walters had heard about the new policy from her participation on the district's community council, where she served as a parent representative. The policy had emerged as part of a faculty discussion about a new evaluation system that explicitly tied student performance to teacher quality. The faculty had deliberated intensely about the potential inequities that might exist in this evaluation system, which relied on standardized assessments administered at the end of the school year. Among the most glaring disparities involved class composition, especially Mrs. Brent's class. Westbrook Elementary, like many public schools, served a community that was mostly supportive. For the majority of parents, that support manifested in their ensuring that their children arrived at school prepared to learn. Attendance at school events was also generally good.

However, a handful of parents were exceptionally engaged in school activities. This was primarily beneficial because these parents supported the school by raising funds for materials and supplies, organizing evening events, and assisting teachers with a variety of in-class and extra-curricular activities. Consequently, this small group of parents was also very knowledgeable about, and well-acquainted with, the teachers in the building. They knew which teachers took classes on field trips, and which ones didn't. And, naturally, these parents wanted their children to have the opportunity to participate in as many educational experiences as possible. In truth, he could hardly blame them.

Unfortunately, one result of allowing parents to request specific teachers had been outrageous disparities in class composition. The children of all of the parents who had leadership roles in the school community seemed to be in the same classes. Victor knew that standardized assessment scores consistently corresponded to socioeconomic status, and, since these parents tended to represent the higher end of the socioeconomic scale of district families, these students were likely to score better on standardized assessments – regardless of the quality of instruction. The faculty members understood this and supported his decision to eliminate parent requests; however, he had a sense that some of the favored teachers were less than thrilled.

"Mr. Romero?" Jo Ann Walters' voice interrupted Victor's thoughts. "Surely you won't deprive Joelle of the chance to be in the spring musical. Only Mrs. Brent's class participates with the fifth graders, so if she doesn't have Mrs. Brent, she can't be in it. I know it's almost a year away, but Joelle has been practicing songs already – with her older sister."

Victor suppressed a sigh and faced the concerned parent, trying to think about how he could best address the problems she raised. As he prepared to speak, she clasped her hands in front of her and met his gaze.

"Mr. Romero, I'm not sure if you know about this, but I just turned in my petition to run for school board. I have the support of the parent community council, as well as the chamber of commerce. And you know that those constituents pretty much guarantee a victory in this district. Now, I don't expect you to change the policy for me. But maybe you might consider making an exception. Just this once."

CASE STORY 4D: DISTRICT LEADER

Jim McMaster had recently completed a state-sponsored Future Superintendents Academy aimed at preparing educators interested in pursuing that position. Jim, who had been nominated for this training program by his current superintendent, had spent three weeks in the summer plus several weekends during the school year attending the academy. He finished in May and was now considering applying for superintendent vacancies in districts similar to, but perhaps smaller than, the one where he currently worked. He was confident that the academy's coursework on topics such as communications, school finance, human resources, and school change had prepared him well for a district leadership position.

Jim was in his fourth year as the assistant superintendent for curriculum in the Pine Hill Central School District, located in an upper middle class suburban district near a major city in the Midwest. Pine Hill was not unlike the districts Jim and his wife, Chloe, had graduated from nearly 20 years ago. The student population was about 6,500, divided among four elementary schools, one middle school, and one high school. Ninety-seven percent of the students were white and less than 7% of students qualified for the Federal "Free and Reduced Lunch" program. Poverty was definitely not an issue at Pine Hill.

In addition, reports filed by the high school counseling center indicated that over 90% of Pine Hill's graduates went on to college, with a significant number attending top tier universities. Jim's two children, Amy and Leif, attended Baker Elementary, which was regarded as the best of the four elementary schools. Chloe worked from their home, designing electronic patient record systems for medical practices, but she did have to travel outside of the area from time to time to meet with clients. Jim and Chloe had discussed Jim's career aspirations. They hoped that he might be able find a position in a nearby school district; one similar to Pine Hill.

CHAPTER 5

Prior to his current position, Jim had served as an elementary principal for several years in Ardley, a smaller but equally affluent neighboring suburban district. He had begun his career as a fourth grade teacher at Ardley, a position he'd held until he had been appointed principal.

It was mid-July and Jim was sitting in his office preparing a staff development report when he received an unexpected phone call.

"Jim, my name is Wayne Oswald and I help boards of education recruit and select superintendents. I understand you recently finished the Future Superintendents Academy. In fact, I spoke with the folks who were the lead instructors in the latest session and they tell me you were among the brightest, best-prepared candidates. Did you enjoy the academy?"

"Dr. Oswald!" Jim began, "I've heard your name mentioned many times, but I don't believe we've met. It's an honor to speak with you. Thanks for calling and, yes, it was a great experience – one that I was glad to participate in. The readings were informative and the interactions with my colleagues were invaluable. I also enjoyed reflecting on the experience during my three-hour drive home. I learned a lot... and I made many good friends."

"Jim, please call me Wayne. I'm happy to hear that you've grown from these experiences. Here's why I'm calling: do you think you're ready to become a superintendent?"

Initially, Jim had presumed that Wayne Oswald might be calling him to inquire about his impressions of the academy. Admittedly, the possibility that Wayne might be inviting Jim to apply for an opening had crossed his mind; even so, hearing the question aloud was a bit unnerving. He hadn't expected things to move quite this quickly.

"Well, Wayne, yes. I think I'm ready to become a superintendent. In fact, my wife and I have discussed the kind of district I might want to start in. We are looking for a –"

Dr. Oswald interrupted.

"Jim, I would like to hear more about your career aspirations, but let me be very clear. Most superintendents don't start out in the job of their dreams. "Dream" jobs are usually in high performing districts that pay well. They attract the best candidates – people with extensive experience. Generally, folks who aspire to be superintendents have to work their way up to their dream jobs, moving two or three times, and developing a successful track record. So, let me tell you a little bit about the job I'm calling you about."

Wayne Oswald went on to describe the Wollcallen Valley Central District.

"It's about 15 miles southwest of where you work. The board hired me to help them find the next superintendent. As you may know, this is a small, first-ring suburban district, with an enrollment of about 1,200 students. They have a K-8 elementary/middle school and one high school. The population is diverse, increasingly so, and the district is feeling the challenge of having to meet the needs of all its students. Many come from single parent families that tend to be transient. The district has a high rate of poverty and the local tax base is not strong – nothing like Pine Hill's. Academic performance is generally below similar schools in the state and has declined over the last five years.

"Now, don't get me wrong, Jim. I don't want to appear negative. I'm just laying out the big picture here. Despite all this, the community seems very satisfied with the schools, especially with the athletic programs. The school board wants to improve academic performance and has directed me to recruit candidates who have strong instructional leadership experience. And that is where you seem to be a really good fit. Residency is not required and the salary, for a small district, is competitive. I think it's a great opportunity. What do you think? Does it sound interesting?"

This was certainly not the type of district Jim and his wife had envisioned, but Wayne Oswald's points seemed well made. Jim knew that he had to start somewhere to build a record of success before he could secure a position in a more prestigious school district. And he could probably commute to Wollcallen Valley, which meant that his children could remain at Baker Elementary. That would help alleviate Chloe's concerns.

Suddenly aware that Wayne Oswald was awaiting his response, Jim answered, "Yes Wayne, I think I'm interested."

"Great. Please look over the application procedure on the district's website and send your materials to me within two weeks. We'll talk soon. If you have any questions, don't hesitate to contact me."

After several discussions with Chloe, Jim applied for the position and was granted an interview with the seven-member school board. The board consisted of two stay-at-home parents, an accountant, a physician, two attorneys, and a vice president for human resources at an area hospital.

The interview went well and Jim was invited back for a full-day visit to the district including interviews with seven separate focus groups – students, parents, teachers, support staff, principals, central office administrators, and community leaders.

From Jim's perspective, the most challenging group was the community leaders. Of all the focus groups, he felt that they were the least cohesive. Each represented a separate constituency. Jim struggled to find common ground with, and among, them. He noted group members from area businesses, the local newspaper, elected officials, senior citizens, and major civic organizations including those from the Black and Latino communities. In other words, the composition of the community leaders group was very different from the composition of the school board.

The parent group was also challenging. Parent representatives were racially diverse, in contrast to the all-white board of education, administration, and faculty. In fact, the only employee of color Jim had met was the weekend custodian at the elementary school. During the interview, one parent identified sports as a high priority, while another asked Jim how he would meet the needs of families whose children required after-school care. A third asked how Jim would improve the high school's graduation rate and ensure that students had opportunities to attend college. The last parent asked about Jim's experience working with students with disabilities.

Jim felt that his interviews had gone well, and was pleased to be offered the position. After some negotiation, he agreed to a three-year contract that was set to begin on November 1.

In early October, Jim met with the board president, Amy Weingarten. During their conversation, Amy shared the board members' expectations for Jim. These expectations included engaging parents and the community in discussions about improving academic performance.

Funds were scarce, noted the board president, but the board expected Jim to move swiftly to build support among the various constituencies to focus existing resources more directly on initiatives and strategies that would increase academic performance. This, she suggested, could mean reducing the sports program and shifting resources to academics. The board was open to ideas.

It was clear that the board wanted to improve student performance, but Jim found the charge to include the community to be a bit daunting. He had no experience working with diverse community groups. In fact, the two districts where he had worked – Ardley and Pine Hill – always enjoyed broad support for high academic performance. And there had been no discussion in the Future Superintendents Academy about strategies for building community relations with diverse stakeholders.

Jim realized he had less than a month to put together a plan to engage parents and community members in building support for the board's goal. How could he do this? How would he go about selecting parents and community representatives? What might be the pitfalls of the selection process? And how could he be sure the process would work?

Jim felt profoundly unprepared for the task.

REFERENCES

Betts, F. (1992). How systems thinking applies to education. Educational Leadership, *Improving School Quality*, November, *50*(3), 38–41.

Cowan, R.J., Swearer, S.M., and Sheridan, S.M. (2004). Home-school collaboration. Educational Psychology Papers and Publications, Paper 18. http://digitalcommons.unl.edu/edpsychpapers/18.

Davies, D., Henderson, A.T., Johnson, V., and Mapp, K. (2006). Beyond the bake sale: the Essential guide to family-school partnership, New York, The New Press.

DuFour, R. and Eaker, R. (1998). The role of parents in a professional learning community. Professional Learning Communities at Work: Best Practices for Enhancing Student Achievement. National Educational Service, Bloomington, IN. ASCD, Alexandria, VA.

Epstein, J.L., Sanders, M.G., Simon, B.S., Salinas, K.C., Jansorn, N.R. and Voorhis, F.L. (2002). School, family, and community partnerships: Your handbook for action (2nd ed.). Thousand Oaks, CA: Corwin.

Senge, P. (1990). The fifth discipline: The art and practice of the learning organization. New York: Doubleday.

CHAPTER 6

STANDARD 5: ACTING WITH INTEGRITY, FAIRNESS AND ETHICS

Standard 5: *An education leader promotes the success of every student by acting with integrity, fairness, and in an ethical manner.*

Functions:

A. *Ensure a system of accountability for every student's academic and social success*
B. *Model principles of self-awareness, reflective practice, transparency, and ethical behavior*
C. *Safeguard the values of democracy, equity, and diversity*
D. *Consider and evaluate the potential moral and legal consequences of decision-making*
E. *Promote social justice and ensure that individual student needs inform all aspects of schooling*

The numerous responsibilities of educational leaders often make it difficult to maintain priorities consistent with a distinct philosophical approach – especially one that requires meaningful involvement with a variety of stakeholders. Certainly, it is easier to make a decision unilaterally than to seek and weigh input from colleagues, students, and community members. Despite the challenges of collaboration, educational leaders must strive to act in ways that reflect the highest standards of integrity, fairness, and ethical behavior. Throughout this text, case stories are presented in order to challenge simplistic notions of right and wrong.

INTEGRITY

Integrity is a complex concept; it incorporates both personal and moral considerations as well as consistency of thought and action. Personal integrity is often likened to purity; however, integrity is grounded in moral actions that relate to the common good and what is best for society, as a whole. Integrity, then, involves adherence to a multilayered set of values. Dunn (2009) describes it as follows:

> What we know of integrity so far is that it requires *coherence among a set of moral values, with this set of moral values having consistency with a set of social values, and that integrity further requires congruence between an*

agent's behavior and this set of moral/social values over time and across social context(s) (Emphasis in original). (p. 104)

To act with integrity, then, requires making explicit connections among personal beliefs, moral values, and the common good. This is much more nuanced than the more superficial understanding of integrity as requiring a sense of constancy between a leader's actions and words.

To clarify the critical nature of integrity as a component of leadership, Holloman, Rouse and Farrington (2007) place the concept of integrity in a concrete context:

In construction the integrity of a beam is vital to the building in which it belongs. Another word for integrity is incorruptibility. The strength of the building is only as strong as the integrity of the weakest beam. A corrupt beam with impairments or flaws will quickly be tossed in the trash pile before it becomes a part of the design.

Perhaps the greatest challenge that administrators face is maintaining the integrity of the school organisation. (p. 440)

Focusing on developing a theoretical foundation for integrity, Dunn (2009) makes the following claims.

Persons of integrity exhibit high regard for

...a consistent set of significant moral principles.

...maximizing net social benefits.

...realizing their personal ethical ideal.

...fair treatment of others.

...nurturing caring relationships. (pp.117–120)

It is evident that the development of integrity is reflected in everything an educational leader says and does. Integrity is a quality that transcends institutional walls or the roles defined by an organization; it unites words, actions, and principles in a cohesive whole in which the moral character of a person is enacted.

FAIRNESS

Fairness is a deceptively simple concept, typically illustrated in terms of an even division of property, attention, or opportunity. In reality, however, fairness and equivalence are very different ideals resulting in vastly different consequences. On the surface, application of fairness implies equality, uniformity, and correspondence – that is, the idea that fairness is analogous to sameness. This simplistic characterization of the notion of fairness, however, ignores the human component, most particularly with respect to diversity.

In short, being fair does not mean treating every person and every incident with the same consequences. If fairness merely required consistency, there would be no need for leaders to concern themselves with integrity, ethics, or principles; leaders could simply consult a handbook to find the "correct" response. In practice, educators understand and appreciate that there is no "one size fits all" strategy for working with people. Therefore, it is essential to consider the personal, social, and moral context in which decisions are made. Complicating matters is the reality that decisions themselves are not made in a vacuum. In fact, for leaders to act with fairness requires them to consult past practices, examine present conditions, and predict future consequences relative to administrative decisions.

The apparent simplicity of the concept of fairness is particularly relevant in the current political context, which is focused on assessment-based measures of accountability.

> Recently, some scholars have argued that standards and assessments theoretically can be aligned with multicultural and culturally relevant education but that in practice they often are not (Bohn & Sleeter, 2000; Kornhaber, 2004). Unfortunately, the majority of standards and assessments that have been employed in schools have served to reinscribe and reproduce the status quo. These practices are veiled under the banner of meritocracy and equality in that they are touted as being fair – in this case, the idea of fairness actually serves to obscure structural and persistent inequities. (Brayboy, Castagno, & Maughan, 2007, pp. 170–171)

Gutierrez (2007) suggests a broader perceptual framework that provides a more accurate representation of the concept of fairness. "The 'sameness as fairness' framework must be replaced with a race-, class-, and gender-conscious equity framework that will make such inequities visible and a humanist vision of education a reality" (p. 121).

ETHICS

The qualities of integrity and fairness both speak to the larger concept of ethics – another term that is historically multifaceted. Philosophically, ethics is often linked to morality: what is right and what is wrong. Such distinctions, again, may appear forthright; however, when they are placed in various contexts, distinctions often blur. The National Education Association (2009) presents its code of Ethics through two principles:

PRINCIPLE I

Commitment to the Student

The educator strives to help each student realize his or her potential as a worthy and effective member of society. The educator therefore works to stimulate the spirit of inquiry, the acquisition of knowledge and understanding, and the thoughtful formulation of worthy goals.

PRINCIPLE II

Commitment to the Profession

The education profession is vested by the public with a trust and responsibility requiring the highest ideals of professional service.

In the belief that the quality of the services of the education profession directly influences the nation and its citizens, the educator shall exert every effort to raise professional standards, to promote a climate that encourages the exercise of professional judgment, to achieve conditions that attract persons worthy of the trust to careers in education, and to assist in preventing the practice of the profession by unqualified persons. (n.p.)

While these principles are worthy of application, there are times when ethical aims may conflict. Suppose, for example, a leader determines that the means through which students are assessed contradict the goal of fostering students as effective members of society. Can a leader subvert the aims of policies if students' interests are not being served? Is it ethical for a leader to support policies that perpetuate inequality?

Such essential, unanswerable questions form the foundation of ethical inquiry that is critical to reflective practice.

CASE STORY 5T: TEACHER LEADER

"Aiden! Got a second?"

John F. Kennedy High School principal Aiden Raul briefly considered tallying the number of times per day he heard this question, but decided the result would probably depress him. He pushed the thought away and smiled toward the doorway, waving the speaker, Doreen Esteves, into his office.

With a gesture, Aiden invited Doreen to sit across from him at the conference table. Whenever possible, Aiden avoided establishing dialogues with his faculty members when he was seated behind his desk. It was just one concrete way that he embraced a participatory leadership philosophy. He knew that every action he took represented a decision, and sitting at a table, rather than across his impressive oak desk, was intended to minimize the power disparity inherent in his role as principal. Sensitive to the changes in communication that tend to emerge from various power dynamics, Aiden was vigilant about seeking a climate of mutual respect in every interaction with students, teachers, parents, community members, and other administrators.

"Thanks," Doreen sighed as she sat down across from Aiden. "I really appreciate your time."

She reached for the large canvas bag that she had set on the floor beside her and removed a manila folder. "I hate to be the bearer of bad news, but I knew you'd want to hear directly from the committee."

Aiden glanced at the folder that Doreen had set on the table. The tab read "Professional Development." Doreen had volunteered to chair the committee that planned the annual staff development day. In her tenth year at the high school, she had understood the importance of the work involved in this task, but she had been considering taking on additional leadership positions in the district and thought this venture might be a good way to sample the experience.

A reliable, hard-working and talented teacher, Doreen had established positive relationships with teachers, support staff, and administrators at JFK High. In addition, she had a stellar reputation among students and parents – a reputation enhanced by her active participation in high-profile activities: she served as senior class advisor and as faculty representative for the Parent-Teacher Organization. Doreen's classroom expertise and her experience organizing numerous school functions had contributed to Aiden's appreciation of her skills and dispositions. And Doreen was truly grateful for Aiden's supportive, transparent, participatory leadership style. She knew that Aiden always put students first, and that he believed in seeking consensus through genuine dialogue – not handing down authoritarian decisions.

Doreen appreciated Aiden's approach, in part, because her first two years at JFK High had been very different; the principal had been a tyrannical, egomaniacal bully who had terrorized students and faculty alike. The culture of the school had been more like a prison than an educational institution. Everyone had been focused on avoiding the principal's wrath – which erupted unpredictably – and even teachers had known it was best to hunker down and stay away from any action that might attract attention. Under the previous principal, teachers had learned to resist taking risks and leadership roles because these led to only two possible actions on the part of the principal. If the initiative was successful, he took credit; and if the initiative failed, he assigned blame.

Aiden had worked hard to change this toxic culture. He had struggled to build trust, to develop and reinforce a sense of collective responsibility, and to create a collaborative community dedicated to consensus-based decision-making. Over the course of the past eight years, and helped along by the retirements of a few particularly oppositional faculty members, Aiden's efforts had succeeded. Communication was open. Teachers felt valued. And it seemed as though the whole school benefited from the shared decision-making model.

"So," Doreen opened the folder, "there have been some interesting responses to our staff development day plans. As you know, representatives on the planning committees went back to their departments at their meetings last Monday. Of course, it was supposed to a formality, since our plans are relatively complete, but the science department came up with a brilliant idea and, over the last few days, everyone's been talking about it. In fact, I made an initial contact with the consultant who would lead the activities, and she is available – and she's in very high demand, so we are really lucky."

"Hold on just a second, Doreen," Aiden's face was friendly, but his voice was tight. "Are you talking about the staff development day scheduled for next month – three weeks from now?"

"Yes! I know that it's short notice, but it's definitely manageable...and exciting. I have never seen the entire faculty so energized about professional development.

All four core subject departments are on board, and even art, music, and physical education teachers are enthusiastic. This is an amazing opportunity to bring the faculty together around a pedagogical initiative!"

Aiden tried to hide his reaction, which fell well short of enthusiasm. It was certainly true that such widespread support for a staff development endeavor was rare; however, plans for this year's activity had been developed through committee consensus and finalized weeks ago. As a member of the committee, Aiden had witnessed and participated in numerous meetings and conversations about the professional development day, and had been instrumental in supporting the plans that had emerged. Moreover, at the last district administrative cabinet meeting, he had reported the details of his building's plan to the superintendent, assistant superintendent, and other building administrators. Even if he endorsed this last-minute change, he wasn't sure how it would be perceived by his administrative colleagues – especially since the other buildings' principals had *mandated* staff development activities based on analyses of standardized assessment results.

Stalling for time, Aiden glanced at the documents in Doreen's folder.

"What's this?" he asked, pointing at a spreadsheet – a format that was conspicuous in the sheaf of papers.

Doreen pulled it from the folder, smiling. "Well, I know how you feel about participatory leadership and the importance of encouraging democratic dialogue so, when this idea was suggested by members of the science department, I took it upon myself to organize a vote, so that everyone's voice could be heard. Look!" Doreen continued, pointing at a highlighted cell on the bottom of the spreadsheet. "The results are unambiguous: 100% of our teachers agree with the new plan. I knew that you would appreciate these data."

Aiden leaned back in his chair, hoping to conceal his reaction and buy some time to think. Just then, the homeroom bell sounded and Doreen rushed to gather her things.

"Thanks so much, Doreen, for your leadership on this," he said. "Let's meet later today to discuss this further."

CASE STORY 5B: BUILDING LEADER

It had taken about three years, but now the full impact of the financial crisis that gripped the nation was being felt by the Crofton Central School District. Located in the state's "Technology Corridor," the once-tiny hamlet of Crofton had grown during the so-called "dot com era" from a sleepy bedroom community of barely a thousand residents to a sprawling township of over thirty thousand.

Thanks to a series of tax breaks for businesses that had agreed to set up shop in the "corridor," the region had experienced a 20-year period of unbridled growth – in tech-related businesses, in job creation, in hiring, in population growth, and, finally, in the construction of new homes.

This, in turn, had led to an explosion in the student population as the tiny Crofton Central School District, once consisting of a single K-6 building and a

7-12 junior/senior high school, had added six elementary schools, three middle schools and two high schools within that 20-year period.

The housing boom had provided a tax base that made Crofton the envy of the region. Each new school was a showcase of modern architecture and, over the years, the various boards of education supported a wide range of innovative curricular and extra-curricular programs: Crofton's marching band was the best in the state; its swimmers regularly finished first, second and third in state meets; and its tennis team benefitted from a dome which provided its players with year round access to courts.

But that was then.

In recent years, the dot com economic bubble burst – as did the housing bubble. Businesses closed in Crofton, employees lost their jobs, and owners of hundreds of homes discovered that they owed much more than their homes were worth, a situation commonly referred to as being "upside down" in a mortgage loan.

As the population shrank, along with the tax base, the Crofton Board of Education began to cut its budget. At first, the cuts did not seem dramatic, but each year, more and more of what had made Crofton unique was disappearing. And over this same time period, the board of education, which during the economic boom had been filled with pro-student, pro-parent trustees, now contained a majority of members who had swept into office under a "fiscal responsibility" platform. Their first act was to eliminate all of the modified sports teams – the middle school 7th and 8th grade teams that had served as feeders for the junior varsity teams. Next, the board cut a range of extra-curricular activities such as the archery club, the Mandarin Chinese club, the Crofton Bloggers, and the Amnesty International club.

The most recent budget eliminated the stipends of faculty who advised all the remaining extra-curricular activities. The belief of this self-labeled "fiscally responsible" board was that teachers, as part of their regular duties, should volunteer time after school to serve as advisors for various clubs and organizations.

As a result, community members split into two camps: one side saw this move toward austerity as nothing less than the dismantling of their once-outstanding school district. The other side felt that fiscal sanity had finally returned to the district and that these measures were necessary in order to control spending. Members of the board of education responded to concerns raised by parents with a consistent refrain: "We're broke and we can't afford to continue funding at the current level." They noted that when times were good, programs expanded, but now that times were bad, it was incumbent on them to make cuts. Board members publicly compared the fiscal situation at Crofton to that of any business where "belt tightening" was necessary.

In response to parental concerns about the cuts in the extracurricular program, and in light of the board's elimination of stipends, the superintendent (following a long Executive Session with the board) decided to ask all current extracurricular advisors to continue their positions on a voluntary basis. The specific request was to be made through the building principals who, the superintendent reasoned, had the closest relationships with the teachers.

North Crofton Senior High School principal, Jed Farris, had just returned to his office after a lengthy Administrative Council meeting with the Crofton superintendent. Jed attended these bi-monthly meetings along with the principals from the district's other schools. It was at today's meeting that the superintendent had revealed the board's proposal to have advisors serve in a voluntary capacity (with no stipends) until the fiscal crisis ended. At the meeting, Jed had listened to the board's perspective as presented by the superintendent.

The superintendent had ended the meeting with these words: "Look, we can't *make* anyone be an advisor without pay, but we can certainly ask them to consider working as advisors for just one year – and, with any luck, this crisis will pass and stipends will be reinstated."

He quickly added: "And be sure to remind your teachers that, if they agree, it will be a very positive public relations move for them, especially with contract negotiations coming up this spring."

The superintendent's words were echoing in Jed's mind as he settled into his office. It was well after 3:00 p.m. and the school, with the exception of custodial activity, was virtually empty.

Jed was surprised to hear someone approaching his office door.

"Hey, you survived another Administrative Council meeting! Congratulations!" Mock excitement was evident in the remark made by Alycia Marcov, North Crofton's assistant principal. She knew that Jed dreaded the twice-a-month Administrative Council meetings, preferring to spend each day at North Crofton where he felt at home interacting with teachers, students and staff. Jed recognized these meetings as a necessary evil, but he was always taken aback by the complex interpersonal and institutional politics that seemed to permeate decisions made at the district level. He had made up his mind long ago: he was happy at the building level and would not pursue a district level administrative position.

"Yeah, we solved several global crises today," Jed tried to return her banter. But his tone was forced and Alycia, who grown to know Jed well during the six years they had worked together, sensed it immediately.

"What happened? You sound awful, and you don't look too good either," she said.

"Well," said Jed, "you know all those rumors about how faculty advisors should continue on a voluntary basis? Guess who has been directed to make the personal contacts?"

Alycia was stunned: "Don't tell me…"

"Yep," said Jed, "at least for our school, you're lookin' at him." Jed dropped into his chair, his feelings mirrored by his posture.

"So, let me get this straight," said Alycia. "The board of education comes up with this money-saving scheme, they tell the superintendent to make it happen, and he directs the building principals to do the dirty work. Unbelievable!"

"Welcome to my world," said Jed.

"Look," said Alycia, "I'm here to help. Is there anything you want me to do?"

Jed stared off at the faculty parking lot which now held a total of three cars. "I really don't know where to begin. First, I don't believe that people should work for nothing and I don't believe that I should be the one asking them to do so. If this is such a brilliant idea, why doesn't the superintendent or the board come here and make a personal plea?"

Jed wasn't finished. "And another thing: has anyone given thought to the power relationship in this situation?"

Alycia looked puzzled. "What do you mean?"

"Okay, I'm the principal, right? I'm afraid that some of the staff members I speak with will be intimidated into agreeing to the voluntary assignment, especially the newly hired ones who aren't tenured. Who's going to say 'no' to the principal?"

Alycia began to study the same parking lot. "I see your point... but you *have* to meet with each advisor, right? Right, Jed? I mean, you've been directed to do so by the superintendent."

Jed shifted his gaze from the parking lot to Alycia's face. He seemed to have made up his mind.

CASE STORY 5D: DISTRICT LEADER

Julie Taylor was enjoying her first weeks as the new Assistant Superintendent for Human Resources in the highly regarded Spaulding Lake School District when she received a call late Friday afternoon from the high school principal, Andre Gleason.

"Julie, I hate to drop this on you just before the weekend, but I have situation here I want to make you aware of."

When Julie heard the phrase "I have a situation here...," she reached for the nearest piece of paper and began taking notes.

The high school principal began to describe a meeting he had just had with a student named Linda Brookings who was a varsity cheerleader in her junior year at the high school. "It was a short meeting," he said. "She basically said that Steve Michaels, our varsity football coach, was more or less sexually harassing her. Those were her words: 'more or less.'"

"What, exactly, did she mean when she said she was being 'more or less' sexually harassed?" asked Julie.

"Well, that's what made the conversation so strange," said Andre. "When I pushed for some specifics, she said something like, 'It doesn't really matter. I just wanted to let you know that it happened.' She said she just wanted me to be aware of it, but not do anything. Personally, I don't think it's a case of sexual harassment, but since you're the complaint officer, I thought you should know about it even though we probably don't need to pursue the matter."

Julie responded, "Andre, as the complaint officer I can't just *do nothing*. Let me think about this and I will be in touch with you on Monday with a strategy."

Julie was just beginning her second month as the assistant superintendent, having been recently appointed to the position after serving five years as the high school principal in a nearby school district. Despite her lack of experience in the position, she understood the seriousness of any allegation of sexual harassment.

The first thing she did was review the district's sexual harassment policy. Though she was familiar with the language, certain sections now jumped out at her:

Sexual harassment is a violation of law and stands in direct opposition to district policy.

In order for the Board to enforce this policy, and to take corrective measures as may be necessary, it is essential that any student who believes he/she has been a victim of sexual harassment in the school environment, as well as any other person who is aware of and/or who has knowledge of or witnesses any possible occurrence of sexual harassment, immediately report such alleged harassment.

Upon receipt of an informal/formal complaint (even an anonymous complaint), the district will conduct a thorough investigation of the charges.

All complaints should be referred to the district's complaint officer, the Assistant Superintendent for Human Resources.

A number of issues began running through her mind. She was aware that Steve Michaels was a high school football icon. His teams always boasted a winning record and the Spaulding Lake High School football team had won the state Class V championship 3 of the last 5 years. She was also aware that he was the brother of the district's board of education president, Don Michaels, a well-respected local business owner who was hoping to use his experience as board president as a stepping stone to a seat on the county legislature. Don was largely responsible for the forced resignation of the previous superintendent and had led the effort to use a prominent (and expensive) national search firm to help with the recruitment of the recently appointed superintendent, Dr. Salvatore Moscato.

Julie admired and respected Sal Moscato. He was a highly regarded curriculum specialist, having authored numerous articles and made presentations at national conferences on topics including curriculum alignment, literacy instruction, and using student data to improve instruction.

When Sal had hired Julie, he had wanted her to understand the culture of the board of education she would be serving. He stressed that the board members saw themselves as a "hands-on" type of board and that they expected to have input on any matter – be it big or small. He presented these characteristics as positive. He also told her that the board, consisting of several Spaulding Lake High School alumni, believed that the traditions of the school district, and especially the high school, were to be nurtured and protected.

With respect to the current issue, Julie decided that her first action should be to meet with Sal and tell him what she knew about this situation. When she arrived at his office door, she saw that he was on the phone. She was about to step away but the superintendent saw her, waved her to come in, and gestured for her to sit down. He held up one finger indicating that the phone conversation was almost over.

"I understand. Yes, I know, I know. Discretion's the word. Okay, Don, have a good weekend." And he hung up the phone.

Sal greeted Julie warmly. In the weeks that they had been together as central office administrators, they had developed a strong professional relationship.

"Julie! So, what's up this weekend? Did you close on the new house yet?"

Julie's mind was focused on the matter at hand. "Dr. Moscato, I just received a phone call from –"

"Julie, how many times do I have to tell you? It's Sal, just call me Sal," he said. "Now, tell me about this call."

"We have a situation at the high school that I have to look into. It seems that an 11th grade female student has made a sexual harassment complaint, or something close to it, against Steve Michaels."

Julie began to review her notes aloud for Sal. Before she was finished, Sal interrupted.

"Actually, I'm aware of the situation and was just about to walk over to your office to fill you in. The phone conversation you just overheard was with our board president, Don Michaels, who, as you know, is Steve's brother. Don just informed me that this girl – this Brookings girl – is a bit of 'loose cannon' and, from what I've been told, does not want the matter to be pursued."

Julie was quick to respond. "Sal, it doesn't matter whether the girl is a 'loose cannon' or not; nor does it matter whether *she* wants the matter pursued. State law and board policy leave us no choice. As the sexual harassment complaint officer, it's my responsibility to investigate this matter. Once it's brought to my attention, I have no alternative."

The superintendent leaned back in his chair and seemed deep in thought. After a few seconds he re-established eye contact with his new human resources administrator.

"Julie, you and I both know what Steve Michaels means to this community. And my board president is very interested in seeing this matter go away. The girl has no credibility. None. So, even though I understand your zeal in pursuing this matter, you can't lose sight of the bigger picture. We're both relatively new here and, if we're smart, Spaulding Lake doesn't need to be our last stop. This district can be our springboard to bigger and better things – *if* we are politically astute. Besides, you're closing on the new house and you told me how much your daughter loves Southside Elementary. She's in first grade, right?"

Julie remained silent.

"Look," he said, "do what you have to do, but be careful. My gut tells me that the girl is the problem, not Steve."

Julie left the superintendent's office frustrated and a bit confused. What did Sal Moscato mean by "be careful"?

Though it was getting late, Julie decided to begin her investigation by reviewing Steve Michaels' personnel file. She was startled to discover that two other sexual harassment complaints had been filed against him. Although there were anecdotal records concerning both complaints, it appeared that neither had been thoroughly investigated. In one situation, the female student had graduated a few months after making the complaint. The other student complainant had been placed in an alternative high school for disruptive students.

Julie went next door and asked her administrative assistant, Jim Lester, if he had a few minutes.

"Jim, this is confidential, but I received a call from our high school principal concerning a sexual harassment complaint. Apparently, an 11th grade girl has made an accusation concerning Steve Michaels. And after reviewing Steve's file, I noticed that two other complaints were made against him fairly recently. What can you tell me about these two complaints?"

Jim exhaled loudly. "Julie, we looked at those complaints. They're closed. And you don't need to go there. Everyone knows that a lot of the high school girls are attracted to Steve. He's tall, good looking, and charismatic. From time to time kids get carried away and these complaints are just part of the fallout. You have to respect the culture of the community and the district, *and* you have to respect Steve's position as a teacher, coach, husband, and father. My advice is to do what you have to do to say you complied with the policy. You're a smart woman and I'm sure you'll figure it out."

REFERENCES

Bohn A, and Sleeter C.E. (2000) Multicultural education and the standards movement: A report from the field. *Phi Delta Kappan 82*(2):156–159.

Brayboy, B. M. J., Castagno, A. E., & Maughan, E. (2007). Equality and justice for all? Examining race in education scholarship. Review of Research in Education, 31, 159–194. doi: 10.3102/0091732X07300045.

Dunn, Craig P. (2009). "Integrity matters." *International Journal of Leadership Studies*, 102–126.

Gutierrez, K.D. (2007). "Sameness as fairness: The new tonic of equality and opportunity"

Holloman, Harold L., William A. Rouse and Vernon Farrington. (2007), "Purpose-driven leadership: defining, defending and sustaining a school's purpose." *International Journal of Leadership in Education*, 437–443.

Kornhaber M., (2004). In Handbook of research on multicultural education, Assessment, standards, and equity, eds. Banks J., Banks C. (Jossey-Bass, San Francisco), 91–109.

National Education Association. (2009). Code of ethics. Retrieved from:
http://www.nea.org/home/30442.htm

CHAPTER 7

STANDARD 6: INTERACTING IN AND WITH THE LARGER CONTEXT

Standard 6: A school administrator is an educational leader who promotes the success of all students by understanding, responding to, and influencing the larger political, social, economic, legal, and cultural context.

Functions:

A. *Advocate for children, families, and caregivers*
B. *Act to influence local, district, state, and national decisions affecting student learning*
C. *Assess, analyze, and anticipate emerging trends and initiatives in order to adapt leadership strategies*

INTRODUCTION: BEING "POLITICAL"

School leaders who strive to meet ISLLC Standard 6 are able to see and understand the world outside of the confines of their school or school district. They are aware that education is embedded in a greater society that reflects ongoing changes in the culture. Those changes affect, and are affected by, an endlessly evolving political context.

Given the enormous responsibilities related to school leadership (and this book lays out numerous case stories underscoring those responsibilities), it is understandable that school leaders would focus deeply and exclusively on the challenges in their immediate environments. What school leader has time to delve into local, state and national politics? And, besides, what impact can a school leader have on these matters?

Effective school leaders do not simply "manage" students, teachers, parents, and school personnel: they *advocate* for them. Effective school leaders do not simply react to changes in laws and policies; they take the *initiative* to assess and analyze the political and legal landscape, and anticipate emerging trends in order to *adapt* leadership strategies.

Yet the concept of being "political" is generally viewed distastefully by school leaders. Cuban (2009), using building principals as his case-in-point, explains

> Telling principals that their daily work in schools includes political decisions usually prompts head-shaking and mumbled denials. Principals often view politics with distaste reserved for eating a plateful of broccoli. Most

principals…see their roles as both managerial and instructional and are disgusted by decisions that smell of politicking. (p. 1)

Cuban notes that school leaders actually do engage in politics within the organization virtually every day as they work to influence what teachers, students, and parents do and think. These activities are masked by euphemistic phrases like "public relations," "community awareness," "collaborating with teachers," or "working with concerned parents." But make no mistake, these are all political activities. Rude (2009) explains:

The negative connotations of 'politician' are quite understandable, but should not take away from the appreciation of political work in general. Salesman, also, have a political job. Managers have a political job. Indeed, a great many jobs have a political component (p. 4).

WHY POLITICS MATTERS: STAKEHOLDERS AND POWER BROKERS

Educational leaders know that schools have numerous and often contradictory purposes. It is because of these inherent contradictions that the need for political awareness and advocacy manifests. For example, as a society, we agree that children should: be obedient – yet we want them to be critical, independent thinkers; learn knowledge from the past – yet have current, marketable skills; learn to cooperate – yet be able to compete in school and later in life; focus on the "basics" – yet be given access to a wide range of courses and extracurricular opportunities.

It could be argued that virtually *all* discussions and debates at the local, state, and national levels spring from some aspect of these contradictory educational purposes. The ebb and flow of these discussions and debates are made possible through the actions of various *stakeholders* and *power brokers*. It would be a mistake to use these terms interchangeably because there are interesting distinctions between the two.

A stakeholder is defined as "a person or group not owning shares in an enterprise but affected by having an interest in its operation, such as an *employee, customer, or local community*" (Dictionary.com, 2009, italics added). For school leaders, the "customers" are generally considered the students and parents, while the "community" would represent, for example, the residents/taxpayers.

In contrast, a power broker is defined as "a person with power and influence, especially one who operates behind the scenes; a person who is important by virtue of the people or votes they control." The definition also notes that a power broker who does you a favor will expect you to return it" (Dictionary.com, 2012).

Senior citizens in any community represent a unique stakeholder group. By definition, they are stakeholders because they live in the community and pay taxes. They may very well have grandchildren living in the school district.

When it comes to voting, senior citizens are exerting more influence than ever before. It is estimated that they comprise up to 65% of all voters in many elections

(Rosborg, 2007). But Rosborg also points to a much broader swath of stakeholders and powerbrokers that a school leader should take into consideration:

> A school leader has to look carefully at the local community to see who else carries the greatest influence. This influence could be from parent groups, union leadership, a service organization, a wealthy landowner or business person, a local government official, a secretary, a cook, or a custodian within the school system itself.
>
> Working successfully with key stakeholders can also help us achieve our goals. These stakeholders change within the school community as different issues emerge. Sometimes a power broker and a stakeholder are the same person. This often evolves into a pressure group on the school system. *The power brokers and stakeholders have to be identified and communicated with* (italics added), hopefully in a collaborative way. Then a plan has to be developed to gain their support. Leadership is the will, sensitivity, and intelligence to put these pieces of the puzzle together to reach specific goals. (p. 5)

Implicit in inviting stakeholders and power brokers "to the table" is the need for school leaders to develop a welcoming environment characterized by respect for diverse opinions, a desire to listen, and a willingness to share power.

BOARDS OF EDUCATION

School leaders have many responsibilities but among the most important (as noted above) is the ability and willingness to recognize power brokers and stakeholders (Rosborg, 2007). This requires the application of political skills under conditions where the power relationship between the school leader and the power broker/stakeholder may be very different from, for example, that of a principal and a teacher. Rosborg refers to the board of education as the "ultimate local power broker" (p. 5).

It is incumbent upon the school leader, then, to develop a strong knowledge base relative to the local board of education. This means knowing board members' names, their political bases of support, their ideological leanings, the reason(s) they ran for a board position, and any relationships they may have with the school district. For example, does the board member have a relative working in the district or children attending its schools? An effective school leader should know the answers to these questions.

When possible, school leaders should also attend board of education meetings to gain firsthand knowledge of the workings of that group. These experiences will provide a window into the motivations and actions of the board and can provide valuable information when making difficult decisions. Presence at board meetings may also offer opportunities to speak informally with board members and, possibly, build relationships.

THE CULTURAL CONTEXT

In this chapter introduction, school leaders have been encouraged to look at politics from a broader perspective; to see it, not as a necessary evil, but as part of the reality of working in organizations with diverse populations and conflicting purposes.

Lindsey, Robbins, and Terrell (2003) posit the need for culturally competent leaders. They maintain that a school leader must have an understanding of the culture of the school, the school district, and the community in order to be effective. The barrier to this "cultural understanding," note the authors, lies in the presumption of entitlement on the part of school personnel and the school leader. Unfortunately, those who work in schools often see those institutions as belonging exclusively to them.

We suggest that this presumption is a mistake and that it results in a profound unawareness of the need to adapt, of the need to reach out to stakeholders and power brokers, and of the need to listen to other voices.

CASE STORY 6T: TEACHER LEADER

Landon Pathania glanced up at the wall clock and, noting that three minutes remained in the class period, instructed his eighth graders to take out their assignment pads.

"Remember to copy down tonight's homework: page 123, questions 1-20, and page 128, questions 5-15." Landon read these words directly from the whiteboard on which they were written, another prompt to help ensure student compliance. He also walked up and down the rows, checking that the assignment was copied, correctly, into each student's pad.

By the time the bell rang, he was confident that the class was well prepared; if they intended to do the homework, the information would be available. Furthermore, as a backup, assignments were posted on his webpage, which was updated daily.

As Landon dismissed his students, one row at a time, he noticed that his colleague, Mirela Kovic, was waiting just outside his door. He caught her eye and gestured for her to enter. When the last student had exited his classroom, Landon closed the door and smiled at Mirela, who was gazing at him quizzically.

"Wow," she began, "you certainly are *formal* with your students! Do you ever smile?" Mirela shook her head and laughed softly. "If I didn't know you better, I'd think you were, well…*mean*!"

Landon laughed with his colleague, "Have a seat, Mirela. If I have to be 'mean' to get them to learn math, I don't mind at all. In fact, I sometimes enjoy the role. As a coach, you can appreciate that, I'm sure."

Mirela nodded as she slid into a chair. She had selected this time to visit Landon after checking his schedule and noting that it was his planning time.

"Actually, Landon, it's my coaching position that brings me here today."

"Let me guess," Landon knit his brows, feigning deep thought. "Kyle Moseley."

Mirela leaned back in her chair, nodding. "Of course, you're not surprised. He is the only eighth grader on my junior varsity basketball team, so it's pretty obvious, I guess."

"He's a starter, too, isn't he?" Landon reached for his gradebook, anticipating the direction this conversation was going to take.

"Yes, he is," Mirela replied, "but that's not the reason I'm here. The team's record isn't my main concern. Kyle is. If he doesn't stay eligible for basketball, I'm worried that he'll give up on school altogether."

Landon rubbed his chin, considering Mirela's words. As coordinator of middle school eligibility, he was familiar with this dynamic. And, while he was always willing to listen, he had never heard an argument persuasive enough for him to justify allowing an exception to the school's eligibility policy, which required students to maintain a minimum grade of 75 in all their courses in order to participate in any extracurricular activity.

Mirela interrupted his thoughts. "Landon, you know that I feel strongly about the academic achievement of my athletes. In fact, I think that the eligibility policy is an excellent way of motivating students. Lots of students in my physical education classes try harder to keep their grades up because they want to be in the school musical. The policy works really well, for most students."

"But you're thinking that Kyle is somehow different, Mirela? You know that my class is the one that is endangering his eligibility. If the policy is good, why shouldn't it apply to Kyle?"

Mirela took a deep breath and leaned forward. "Landon, you know that Kyle is smart. Really smart. He gets good grades in all his other classes without even studying very much. He has perfect attendance, he's attentive, and he participates. And his scores on tests and quizzes are solid, across the board." She paused, "Even in your class, right?"

"Absolutely," Landon agreed. "His tests and quizzes are not the problem. But he never does his homework." Landon opened his gradebook and scanned the page. "That is not an exaggeration, Mirela. I do mean *never*. He has not turned in a single homework assignment this year. And, since homework is 20% of the grade, his grade is in the 60s, not the 80s, where it could be. Kyle will pass, but he will not be eligible."

"But that's ridiculous!" The words burst from Mirela before she could prevent them and Landon's raised eyebrows reflected his surprise. "I'm sorry, Landon. That was out of line. But Kyle clearly knows the material if he's earning 80s on his tests, right? And he *can't* get his homework done. Between basketball and babysitting, he honestly has no time."

Landon had decided to ignore her outburst. "Mirela, you know as well as I do that we *make* time to do things that matter. I make every effort to support students, to ensure that they can get their work done if they choose to do so. Kyle has chosen not to, and that decision has consequences. Furthermore, Kyle has not registered any concern about his grades at all. I'm surprised that you are advocating for him if he isn't willing to speak on his own behalf."

Mirela pressed her lips together and silently counted to ten. She liked Landon and knew that he was a dedicated teacher.

"The truth is that Kyle doesn't really have a choice, Landon. If he's not in school, he has to take care of his younger brothers and sisters. I don't know if you know this, but he's the oldest of seven children. His father is disabled and his mother works only when Kyle is available to babysit. She lets him play basketball, but even that allowance was a battle. It doesn't seem fair to punish him by deducting 20 points for something he can't control."

Landon deliberated for a few moments, and then closed his grade book. "Mirela, I am very impressed by your commitment to our students, in general, and Kyle, in particular. What I am about to say may not apply in every subject, and I understand that every department has different requirements for homework. As a math teacher, however, I cannot deviate from the 20% homework credit. It is imperative for students to practice if they are going to master the concepts and skills of the course. Your team practices and drills daily, and the same expectations apply to math. Finally, I am certain that if Kyle applied himself to math, his grades would be even better. I would be doing a disservice to him, to his peers, and to the integrity of our policy if I granted an exception in this case. I'm sorry."

Mirela dropped her shoulders and pushed her chair back. She believed that Landon was sorry, and she also believed that he was certain that his decision was correct. As she considered her options to contest the policy, Mirela wondered: How could someone so certain be so wrong?

CASE STORY 6B: BUILDING LEADER

Never in her thirteen years in the Port Washington Central School District (including nearly three years as an elementary school principal) had Clarisse Barton seen anything like it. The amount of criticism being leveled upon public schools and public school teachers by the media, and seemingly every politician locally and nationally, was staggering.

Clarisse avoided watching cable news because whenever the topic was education, she was struck, and sickened, by the comments of so-called experts who did nothing but present simplistic solutions to what she knew were complicated and intractable problems in the field. These were societal problems that schools, as social institutions, might replicate, but certainly did not create.

To Clarisse, it seemed like ages since she had been hired as a new 4th grade teacher at Hill View Elementary School where she had been considered one of the hardest working and most popular teachers on the faculty. After her first year on the job, she became the teacher that seemingly every parent requested. Her former principal, the now retired Jack Mancuso, had been so besieged by parent requests back then that he had devised a lottery system for assigning students to teachers in order to minimize and hard feelings that inevitably arose when parent requests for Clarisse could not be met.

She had loved her fourth graders and had loved the designated curriculum. In addition, Clarisse had served as the faculty liaison with the Hill View Parent-Teacher

Association, was a member of the Superintendent's "Key Communicators Committee," and the Chair of the Elementary Curriculum Committee. Since she was constantly interacting with parents, upper level administrators, community members, and district colleagues from other schools and grade levels, Clarisse was able to see the "big picture" of education in her township.

In all of these venues, Clarisse came across as bright, driven, and diligent. It had seemed natural that her colleagues, and even the venerable Jack Mancuso, himself, had encouraged her to consider a career in school administration.

So, as Clarisse was completing her first decade as a teacher, she had enrolled in the local college and had earned a second master's degree, this one in educational administration. Within a year, Clarisse had been named principal of North Creek Elementary School, Port Washington's other K-6 building. The appointment surprised no one and pleased everyone.

Clarisse now stared at the editorial in the Port Washington *Courier* which praised the new teacher evaluation system that had been negotiated between the state teachers' union and the governor's office, a system based primarily on student performance as measured by standardized tests. The new evaluation system, read the editorial, represented a "fair and accurate measure of teacher effectiveness." The editorial concluded with the words, "This is a great day to be a student."

A separate news article related to the new evaluation system included a quote from the Port Washington Superintendent, "We have confidence that the new evaluation system will enable Port Washington to become a better and more accountable school district." The President of the Port Washington Board of Education was quoted as saying, "If teachers are not getting the job done, we will give them help; but if they continue to flounder, we now have a structure in place to remove them. Our kids deserve highly qualified teachers."

Clarisse felt uneasy about these comments. It was evident that the administration and board of education supported this approach to school reform. Clarisse knew that, as a third year principal, *she* worked for *them* but her knowledge of the nature of schools and schooling, coupled with her deep understanding of this community, told her that teacher competence could not be assessed exclusively by student performance on standardized tests. Ruefully, she thought of the famous quotation by H. L. Mencken: "For every complex problem, there is an answer that is clear, simple – and wrong."

Clarisse was well aware of the negative effects of standardized testing, especially when used in "high stakes" situations. Well, she thought, the stakes just don't get any higher than the threat of losing your job due to poor student performance. As part of her administrative training, Clarisse had become familiar with scholarly literature critical of the misuses of standardized test results. Issues of validity and reliability were always in question, not to mention rampant cheating as had been reported in several states. Yet, the media presented the connection between teacher performance and standardized tests as an almost logical reform initiative. They were proclaiming the success of a flawed measure before anything was even implemented.

She also knew that by focusing on the tests, teachers invariably began to narrow the curriculum; that is, teach to the test. For example, one of the high school history teachers said that the social studies department had been skipping content related to the Presidency of Richard Nixon. "The state tests never ask a question about Nixon – so we just quit covering him," he had said.

Clarisse felt as if she had to do something. After rereading the editorial and the news article, she decided to write a letter to the editor. Someone needs to respond, she thought. Didn't she have a responsibility to use her knowledge and skills to educate the public on this issue? And shouldn't someone speak up on behalf of the students and the teachers who would be most affected by the tests and the evaluation system?

The letter seemed to write itself. It read: *This is in response to your editorial entitled "Reform at Last" which praised the new teacher evaluation system based on student performance on the state's standardized tests. As the principal of North Creek Elementary School, I believe that this initiative is misguided. Standardized tests are a measure of student performance, but just one of an array of measures. How a child performs on a single paper-and-pencil test given once a year over a two-hour period is not a valid measure of that child and certainly not a valid measure of that child's teacher. In addition, research on the effects of standardized testing shows that it narrows the curriculum and results in rote memorization. What's more, it is important to consider what standardized tests do not measure, including qualities such as persistence and love for learning. These tests and the new performance system will not result in greater accountability and they are certainly not "fair and accurate" measures of teacher competence. The way to improve our schools is not a secret. Anti-poverty policies which include an effective pre-school program, good nutrition and health care, involved parents, a child-centered curriculum, and ongoing assessment – along with a strong teacher evaluation system – will work to improve all schools.*

Clarisse printed her letter and sat down to read it. She knew that her opinions were at odds with the media, the superintendent, and the board president but she was as frustrated as she had ever been with the toxic anti-education culture. She briefly considered running the letter past the district's communications officer, but decided against it, guessing that he would probably refuse to allow her to submit it. Clarisse concluded that, on this issue, she would rather ask forgiveness than permission.

She put the letter aside, planning to decide whether to send it the next morning. Sleeping on it was, of course, a good idea, but, she realized she had already made up her mind. Clarisse thought, "I don't work for the superintendent; I work for the kids."

CASE STORY 6D: DISTRICT LEADER

Dr. Betsy Flemming had followed a non-traditional path to her current central office position as Assistant Superintendent for Curriculum, Assessment and Planning, a position she had held for the past five years. Since Betsy had never been a principal or assistant principal, her trajectory was viewed by some as unusual. Nonetheless, she had spent over 20 years in the field transitioning through leadership positions of increasing responsibility. Betsy had recently completed her Ph.D. and, after five years as assistant superintendent, was eager to take on her next position.

Aside from her work, Betsy was often involved in activities she could justify as serving students, her district, and the profession. She trained new school board members, taught administration courses at the university, and had developed a significant network of professional acquaintances. These varied experiences provided her with a unique perspective on education. Betsy was always ready to share stories – of challenges, successes, or needs faced by schools – with anyone who she thought would listen or, even better, who had clout to help.

In the last two years, Betsy had been a runner-up for the position of school superintendent in two different districts. Disappointed with the outcomes, she had sought feedback from the respective search consultants on how to improve her chances.

"Don't change a thing, Betsy," said one consultant. "The board thought you were great; they just went with a safer choice."

"A safer choice?" asked Betsy, "What does that mean?"

"Well," the consultant paused. "Perhaps you come across as a bit too involved. This board wanted someone more traditional – someone whose energy is not spread in so many directions. They wondered if you are really focused on this work – the work of leading a district."

Betsy mulled this over. "Is it true? Am I spread too thin? Am I focused enough?" She struggled to understand how the board could not connect her involvement in a variety of activities *outside* of work as directly influencing the success of the students *inside* her district.

"You were too smart for them," said the second consultant. "Not everyone is such a big thinker. The board is not like you. They are focused on *their* issues, not *the* issues in the bigger context." Again, Betsy struggled to understand how she could be *too* smart, *too* involved and *too* visionary in her thinking. After all, aren't those traits you would expect a school leader to have?

Betsy continued her efforts at work, advancing opportunities for students and teachers. She helped teachers write grants, facilitated regional school district collaborations, and oversaw the establishment of intervention programs in her district.

Outside of work, she remained active in her professional associations, wrote articles on the issues facing public education, and broadened her network. Most importantly, Betsy focused on being able to articulate how her involvement *outside* work was enhancing the overall success of her school district and public education.

Less than a year later, Betsy learned that another local school district would be seeking a new superintendent. She was invited to meet with the search consultant to discuss her qualifications. Betsy was hesitant about applying again. She knew she was not fully challenged in her current position, but she was mindful of the professional impression that might result from another unsuccessful candidacy. Despite her reservations, Betsy agreed to meet with the consultant. She made copies of reference letters along with charts and graphs that showed increases in student performance as a result of her initiatives. She included examples of her increased influence and participation at the local, state, and national levels. Betsy was confident that her materials represented a range of accomplishments which showcased her strengths.

"Wow, Betsy, you are a woman on the move," said Paul Sen, the consultant, after reviewing her material. "You are clearly involved at every level in education."

"I just hope that that's a good thing," said Betsy.

"I certainly would expect so!" responded Paul. "If *you* can't influence and advance a school district, I don't know who can."

Betsy spent the next few weeks researching the district and reflecting on whether or not to apply. She spoke with friends, family, and mentors. She placed a call to Henry Cole, a sitting superintendent and one of her most trusted mentors. Henry had known Betsy throughout her career.

"The work of being a superintendent may bore you, Betsy," he offered.

"Bore me? How can you say that? Think of the connections, think of the influence, think of the possibilities I can bring to the district," responded Betsy in disbelief.

"I am starting to think you are meant for state level or policy level work. Give that some thought." he said. After Betsy hung up the phone, she felt even more unsure about her decision.

Continuing her research on the district, Betsy located a copy of the current superintendent's contract. As she skimmed its contents, she came across an "Other Work" clause that would clearly limit her involvement in some of outside-district professional activities. It read:

13. *Other Work. The Superintendent shall devote his/her full-time skill, labor and attention to the discharge of his/her duties during the term of this Agreement; provided, however, that the Superintendent, subject to the approval by the Board, may undertake consultant work, speaking engagements, writing, lecturing, or other professional duties, and obligations without remuneration, just as long as such activities do not interfere with the full and faithful discharge of the Superintendent's duties and responsibilities as specified herein.*

Reading this, Betsy thought of a recent solicitation from another school superintendent to provide a keynote address to the board of education during its winter retreat. She also thought of her commitment to serve as a board member of three regional civic organizations and her position as vice president of a national staff development association. Betsy winced at the thought of not being able to provide such services. Prior approval? "What business is it of theirs what I do outside of work, as long as I am an effective superintendent?" she wondered.

Seeking a way around this stipulation, Betsy read the vacation clause; perhaps she could use a vacation day to complete such work.

9. g. Vacation Leave. The work year shall consist of twelve months (12) months, from July 1 through June 30, during which the Superintendent shall be entitled to receive fifteen (15) paid vacation days. The Superintendent will not use any of his/her vacation time during any period that school is in session.

Betsy was stumped. Not only would she need to seek approval for any outside involvement, she would be limited as to *when* she could use her vacation time. Only 15 days of vacation. This was less than what she was allotted in her current position. Her conclusion was simple: If I take this job, there is no way I can continue my professional and civic commitments.

Just then, her phone rang. "Hi Betsy; this is Paul Sen, search consultant for Oakville. The posting closes this Friday. Can I expect your application?"

REFERENCES

Cuban, L. (2009). Principals as political actors: facing reality. Retrieved at http//larrycuban.wordpress. com/2009/12/15/principals-as-political-actors-facing-reality.

Dictionary.com (2009). Retrieved at http//dictionary.reference.com/browse/stakeholders.

Dictionary.com (2012). Retrieved at http//dictionary.reference.com/browse/powerbroker.

Lindsey, R.B., Robbins, K.N. & Terrell, R.D. (2003). A manual for school leaders. 2nd Edition, Corwin Press, Inc. A Sage Publication Company, U.K.

Rosberg, J. (2007). School leadership, from What Every Superintendent and Principal Should Know, Rosberg, J., McGee, M., and Burgett, J. (eds) Second edition. The Burgett Group.

Rude, B. (2009). One response to principals as political actors: facing reality. Retrieved at http//larrycuban.wordpress.com/2009/12/15/principals-as-political-actors-facing-reality.

AFTERWORD: LEADING IN THE WORLD

Analysis, discussion and role-play of the scenarios presented in case stories represent the first steps toward becoming an effective, reflective leader. However, they are exercises meant to simulate and expand on *authentic experiences*.

In the contemporary world, educators at all levels face unprecedented challenges; challenges that threaten to undermine the profession. These include the regulation of assessment and instruction, and the narrowing of the curriculum. Increased external control of the processes of education is restricting the capacity of school leaders. Since education is the cornerstone of dynamic democratic processes, it must be maintained. Democratic societies require critical thinkers who can question the status quo. Blind compliance stands in opposition to this model.

Educational leaders are charged to prepare students to thrive in a world that does not yet exist. In that way, we shape the future. Our hope is that the stories in this book illustrate the complexities of leadership in educational settings, and – more importantly – that the analyses will extend understandings in ways that can be applied to everyday situations.

When dilemmas emerge in your own practice, consider how the A-PIE framework might inform decisions and plans, with the goal of continuous improvement in our quest for social justice.